I0491722

# How To Start An Online Business

# The Ultimate Step-By-Step Guide To Starting An Online Business For Single Moms

## KING ARI DANE

# ABOUT THE BOOK

Not every superhero wears a cape, and this statement points to the role of a SINGLE MOM who have chosen to turn their drive into PROSPERITY. The guides in this book will take you through tons of eye-opening opportunities that you can venture into as well as the necessary tools needed to run an online business.

*There is no limitation to what you can achieve, the ONLY limitation is in your mind.*

**Copyright © 2020 KING ARI DANE**

All rights reserved. No part of this guide may be reproduced in any form without permission in writing from the publisher except in the case of brief quotations embodied in critical articles or reviews.

ISBN-9798648742529

# Legal & Disclaimer

The information contained in this book is focused on business, entrepreneurship and market inclined topics.

The content and information contained in this book has been compiled from sources deemed reliable, and it is accurate to the best of the Author's knowledge, information and belief. However, the Author cannot guarantee its accuracy and validity and cannot be held liable for any errors and/or omissions. Also, that the use of the guidance in this guide will lead to any particular

outcome or result or build a successful online business

Further changes and information might be made to this book periodically as and when needed.

Upon using the contents and information contained in this book, you agree to hold harmless the Author from and against any damages, costs, and expenses, including any legal fees potentially resulting from the application of any of the information provided by this book.

This disclaimer applies to any loss or damages caused by the use and application, whether directly or indirectly, of any advice or information presented, whether for breach of contract, tort, negligence, personal injury, criminal intent, or under any other cause of action.

You agree to accept all risks of using the information presented inside this book.

# Table of Contents

# INTRODUCTION

Being a single mom can bring on and even increase emotional and financial hardships. While many single parents are already busy with work and children, some are choosing to add to the frenzy by starting their own business. With the necessary tools available online, single moms are more able to tap into their entrepreneurial spirit and take their financial future into their own hands.

Adding the tremendous focus necessary to start a business while paying attention to your children as a mom is not easy, and careful consideration will have to be taken when approaching this task. Starting an online business may be appealing to a single mom because you can have it all, limitless time with your children, and also making an income to supplement your family.

I believe there are dozens of opportunity out there for you, all you need to do is to TAKE A LEAP. Several single moms have followed this path and had a complete story change. The guides in this book will take you through tons of eye-opening opportunities that you can venture into as well as the necessary tools needed to run an online platform. There is no limitation to what you can achieve, the ONLY limitation is your mindset.

Regardless of your motive to start an online business, whether you want to run a side hustle to make millions along with your corporate job or you are in the clueless state after losing a source of income, whatever state you are in

right now. This is for you. You simply can follow this tested-and-proven advice and take one baby-step after the next until you arrive at your financial destination.

If that sounds too good to be true, you're right. There is indeed a catch, and it's a big one: To be successful in building an online business, you must ignore a lot of conventional wisdom and advice. Whether it's rattling around in your head or someone's telling it to you, most of it is a combination of lies, half-truths, myths, and just plain outdated information on what it takes to be successful online.

Before I depress you too much, I will help you discard a few bogus ideas generated by your brain in the form of self-doubts or beliefs associated with starting an online business. Also, these ideas might be from well-meaning friends or family members. Either way, it's toxic to hold on to this unhealthy piece of information. It is my first task to clear your head of these beliefs so we can go make a bunch of money.

Let's consider these bits of bogus advice to be big Keep Out! Signs on your way to wealth.

*I Don't Have Enough Money*: Oh, and if you think you need a bunch of money to design and manufacture a product, it just isn't so. I'll show you how to create a product for next to no money and for just a little bit of your time, believe it or not.

*It's a Bad Economy*: Let's examine that statement a little more closely. Newspapers, television, and the Internet are indeed full of bad-news stories

every day. That doesn't make it a uniformly bad economy. The ball lies in your court, how you react to the information.

*I Don't Have Enough Time*: You don't need big blocks of time to start an online business. All you need is scraps of time here and there. As a single mom, you might often find yourself stretched for time, energy and money. All you need to do is to be more resourceful and creative when it comes to exploring business opportunities that will not interfere with being a mom. I'm a firm believer that single moms, in particular, should see entrepreneurship as a road to travel. I know there are many reasons why a single mom would say "When would I find the time?" or "Who's going to watch my child while I work?" or "I don't have the extra money to invest in a business." All these are valid ☐uestions but hey, all you need is a commitment. The real trick is to know your very next step to take and to take small actions regularly.

*I'm No Good with Computers*: Can you turn on your computer and use a mouse? Can you read plain text on the screen? Okay then, you're good to go. You no longer need to know any programming to get a perfectly fine web site up and running. You do need to be clear and direct in what you offer people, and that's easy to accomplish, as you'll soon discover

*All the Good Ideas Are Taken*: This sounds like the Roman Governor Julius Sextus Frontinus in around AD 60, who said: "Inventions have long since reached their limit, and I see no hope for further developments. This statement is a lie. Anything can sell off the internet in this millennial age.

9

*I don't have the necessary skills*: Any skills re□uired to start an online business can be learned. All you need is commitment and patience. Also, I promise to help you identify these skills and teach you all you need to know.

*The internet is congested or there's Too Much Competition*: When you offer a new-and-improved dog collar to the market today, you have millions of potentially immediate users, depending on how good your doggie collar is. Here's the excellent news: Most of your competition is not very good at selling dog collars. However, your customer service must be top-notch. It makes good companies stand out and that's the kind of business that sets the blaze on the internet. Savvy marketers have a rule: For fastest revenue growth, look for businesses with an existing, installed base of customers and do the job better. It's smart advice.

In this book, I have compiled all of the information about starting a successful online business that I've collected over time so it can serve others. The book will take you step-by-step through the different aspects you should consider when building an online business to increase your chances of success. The information is presented in a logical se□uence, with each chapter leading to the next. The concepts are not to be taken lightly; I can assure you that seriously considering them as you build your online business will save you time in the long run.

Building a successful online business in your home can let you enjoy your work more, worry less about money, spend more time with family, work on projects you enjoy, and share that success with others, too. Note that reading this book isn't suddenly going to make you $1,000,000. But it will give you

the tools to redesign your career and make the most out of your life as I have. There are no ⬜uick money schemes here. It is important to know that an entrepreneur is a person that creates value. You get paid for the value you bring to the market.

I hope that you enjoy it and that it's helpful to you in creating a life you are happier to live.

# CHAPTER ONE

## ROAD TO HAPPINESS

*"To make yourself happy, pursue your passions & be the best at what you can be. Simplify your life. Take away the clutter. Live on Purpose!"* – *Unknown*

The journey as a single mother isn't an easy ride. Shuttling between work and taking care of your kids are your sole responsibility. Finding the work life balance is an essential skill every single mom should possess to avoid wearing out.

Perhaps you've always wanted to be your own boss, but have never started your own business due to a lack of time, money, or even ideas. Maybe you were held back by the fear of putting yourself or your family at risk.

You have to take deliberate responsibility of your life. Imagine working for yourself, with no one to tell you what to do. You take on the projects that appeal to you most, and feel proud as you watch them grow. You add value to the market while influencing people around you. If this sounds more interesting, then you likely have an entrepreneurial spirit.

However, it has never been as easy to become an entrepreneur as it is today. The Internet has brought down most of the entrance barriers to entrepreneurship. You can start building your business while still working at your regular job and only investing one hour of your time per day. Besides, you have access to a massive goldmine of information to help you succeed: podcasts, books, blogs, etc. You can take advantage of listening to others' experiences, and use this knowledge to build your project faster and safer. The most thing you need is the deep commitment to learning and willingness to put some effort into achieving your goals.

*The Internet has completely changed the game for anyone who wants to have their own business. It's now easier, faster, and cheaper to start and run a business than at any time in history.*

You probably have held about MOMpreneurs. If not, a Mompreneur is someone who takes on two jobs as a mother and as a business owner. Many starts a business that provides flexibility, and that can be done from home, like with an Etsy shop. Others want to start a business with minimal costs, such as a blogging site or iPhone photography. Whatever you decision is, you can be your own boss and achieve success without any regrets. *You are the Boss, Own It.*

THE DIGITAL OPPORTUNITY

With an online business, you can work from wherever you want, whether it be your home, a cafe or a co-working space. You can choose where to live in, your home town or elsewhere and you have the freedom to organize your schedule almost entirely as you wish. No, you won't have to be stuck in a cubicle all day long, eat lunch at the office cafeteria, and spend hours in traffic during rush hour, hit the gym at the same time as everyone else and wait in line for the next available treadmill. Perhaps most importantly, your salary won't be limited to what an employer is willing to provide.

The cost of starting and operating an online business is minimal, so is the financial risk factor. All you need to purchase are a hosting service (about $5/month) and a domain (about $10/year). For the rest, it all depends on the type of market or service you're getting into, but it is possible to start with as little as $100. Pretty incredible, right?

The truth is that the most difficult part of beginning a new endeavor is deciding to do it. You can easily get bogged down with excuses for why your business won't happen. To keep you motivated and on track, here's a list of the Top 8 reasons to start an online business now:

*You can gain financial freedom.* One major incentive for owning any business is the potential for a better income. The Internet offers the opportunity to create your wealth.

*You have unlimited customer reach.* No geographical boundaries exist when you run a business over the Internet. You can choose to sell your products or services within your community, within your own country, or to the entire world.

*It's affordable.* You can now create a web site inexpensively and sometimes for free. The cost to maintain your site, secure products, and cover related expenses is often relatively low. This low start-up cost is especially evident when you compare the start-up costs of online business and a traditional bricks-and-mortar business.

*Your schedule is flexible.* Part-time, full time, year-round, or seasonal; your schedule is up to you when you operate your virtual business. You can work in the wee hours of the night or the middle of the day. An online business affords you the luxury of creating a work schedule that works for you.

*Novices are welcome.* As the Internet has grown, e-commerce (a type of business activity conducted over the Internet, such as sales or advertising) applications have become increasingly simple to use. Although you benefit from having experience with your products or services, the process of offering those items for sale online is easy to understand. You can set up shop with little or no experience under your belt!

*You can start ☐uickly.* From online auctions like eBay to storefronts powered by Amazon.com, the tools that can help get you started are readily available.

*You can expand an existing business.* If you already own a business, the Internet provides you with the most economical and most efficient way to expose your business to a huge new group of customers and increase sales.

*A variety of ideas ☐ualify.* As proven time and again, the Internet supports a broad range of business concepts. Although some ideas are better suited to long-term success, almost all your ideas have potential.

# SUCCESS STORIES: SINGLE MOTHERS, SMALL-BUSINESS OWNERS

Every MOMpreneur face challenges in getting their business started. Now, add in the responsibilities and time demands of being a single mother, and the path gets that much more challenging. But inspiration can often come from those that have experienced such struggles.

Here are a few examples of single moms that have gone on to small business success.

### Be kind to yourself.

Karla Campos, a single mother of three, was included in a recent entrepreneur.com feature by Kate Taylor. Campos is the founder of marketing company Social Media Sass and is also involved in the social media conference Florida Social Con.

She connects entrepreneurship to motherhood because it "is not a 9 to 5 job," she says. "Some days I stay up until 3 a.m. working, and then have to do a 7 a.m. child drop-off at school. Be kind to yourself. Make time for you even if it's just to breathe and smell the air. Kids are going to make messes, they are going to eat your reports and download viruses to your computer. Your best weapon is a sense of humor. Enjoy your single mom entrepreneur life, wear the title proudly. We are superheroes.

### Don't let inexperience stop you.

Melissa Kieling is a mother of three and featured in Taylor's entrepreneur.com story. Kieling developed the Packit Personal Cooler, a lunch bag with a gel lining that can freeze, therefore keeping kids' lunches cold. What started as a small project is now a multimillion-dollar business.

**"Look for inspiration everywhere,"** she says. "Make note of all the things that frustrate you in your daily life, then research creative ways to address those inefficiencies. All it takes is an idea and an Internet connection to create a product that changes the world." Kieling admits she was initially "paralyzed" with fear as she tried to get her business off the ground. "I overcame this by reaching out to other business owners who could connect me to experts in manufacturing, production and sales," she said. "Each key person I met shortened my learning curve and gave me confidence. You'll be pleasantly surprised by how other business owners want to pay it forward and see new upstarts succeed."

*I had to rethink how the business could grow.*

Bianca Whitfield had a challenging road to business success after a divorce. With family support to help look after her young daughter, Whitfield went back to school to pursue her master's degree. She eventually founded an accounting firm, WhitGroup Consulting LLC. In a 2010 story by womenhomebusiness.com, Whitfield describes adjusting to self-employment, including the work-life balance difficulties that single moms often face.

"**You don't work less when you're self-employed, you just get more flexibility with when and where you put in the hours**," writes Whitfield. "My daughter was very sick in the fall with one asthma attack after another. She was in and out of school, back and forth to the doctor, and I was slammed with audits, fourth-quarter financial reports, and a host of other client needs that I just couldn't meet. Things started to unravel, and I had to scale back, get help and work smarter. The business essentially still revolved around me, and I had to rethink how the business could grow.

*Find what works for you.*

Sherry Colbourne is a social-media specialist in Canada who also helps to mentor young entrepreneurs. The schedule demands of being a single mom and starting a business are significant, she says in Taylor's entrepreneur.com story.

"Mompreneurs, more than other entrepreneurs, **need to be disciplined in their relationship with time**," says Colbourne. "When I was a single mom with a growing business, I would wake up at 5 a.m. so I'd be in the right frame of mind to deal with my then-teenage children. Morning conversation and breakfast provided the energy we needed for the day and a sit-down dinner provided the engagement we needed to stay connected. I found the natural rhythms in my business and used them to schedule appointments and work out. There were no marathon workouts for this girl, but half an hour on a treadmill can go a long way to clearing your head and reclaiming your energy. Find what works for you and make yourself one of your priorities!"

*Technical knowledge is not an excuse*

Janice Taylor will be the first to tell you that she's not the doe-eyed Pinterest mom who slaves over intricate cupcakes. Instead, she's a busy, energetic solo mom of two girls while also **running her own tech company** and earning national acclaim in her native Canada.

*Connect with your content*

Taylor, 42, is the founder and CEO of Mazu, **a digital village where parents and kids can connect in a way that's both fun and safe**. She describes the mobile messaging and content app as a "walled garden for our children to not only engage with content that's appropriate and healthy but to engage with us as well as parents, as a family." The company is also partnered with several National Hockey League, National Basketball Association, and Women's National Basketball Association teams to reach kids under the age of 13.

### There is no limitation to what you can achieve

Yalanda P. Lattimore was working three jobs, seven days a week. She held a full-time contracting position at Hewlett-Packard, she worked at Waffle House on the weekends, and she had a third side hustle selling gift baskets online. And she was a Solo Mom to four children.

"I was just like, this can't be my life," she says. So she looked inward and relit a flame that had been burning inside her from a very young age. Lattimore, now 50, wanted to write. She hunkered down in a tiny closet-turned-office and set to work.

**She taught herself how to code and how to build websites in those early days of the World Wide Web**. She began blogging about news and happenings around her native Atlanta. Then she combined it all, and in 2002, DryerBuzz.com was born.

The dishy, socially conscious news site aims to make readers think and debate with topics ranging from success (or lack thereof) in diversity to trying out the raw-diet fad to celebrations of black hair. The site has exploded in popularity.

# CHAPTER TWO

THE ULTIMATE STEP BY STEP GUIDE

There is a proven se□uence of steps you can follow to guarantee your success when you're starting a small business online.

*STEP ONE: CHOOSE A SUITABLE BUSINESS MODEL*

I t is important to clarify before we start, that there is a difference between working on a personal project and building a business. A personal project is carried out solely for satisfaction, it does not require the opinions of others. Basically, the project is all about you. However, when you are building an online business, it is no longer all about you; it is about them. It's about serving an audience, a market, and addressing a need they have expressed.

The primary responsibility of a business is to serve the market. For instance, if you created a travel blog, is your blog a business? The answer is not a simple "yes" or "no." A blog in itself is a personal project, but once you monetize a blog by adding advertising, or by selling your own or an affiliate's products, then you have started a business.

**Overview of online Business Models and Website Monetization**

There are four main approaches when discussing online business models.

*Selling your product through your platform (website)*: This is the most viable and safe approach, in the long run. It re□uires you to create your platform and build your audience.

*Selling others' products on your platform and getting a commission*: This is the most lucrative model within the approach and it is the only one that will grant you the most control to sell your products or services.

*Having others sell your product and giving them a commission*

*Selling others' products on a third-party platform:* For example, reselling products that are not yours on Amazon or eBay and making a profit

The third and the last approach gives you the least control over your income, selling other people's products through a third-party platform. However, these models are not mutually exclusive, and you should use more than one method to generate revenue.

The main online business models according to their investment costs and profitability are classified into four;

Low cost and low profitability; advertising and affiliates

High cost and high profitability; Software and Physical products

Low cost and high profitability; Consulting and Online courses

Personally, I believe it's good to diversify your income sources and choose more than one way to generate revenue. For example, you could use a mixture of selling your products and those of affiliates or offer online courses in addition to your coaching or consulting services.

There are many ways to make a living online: monetizing a blog, offering consulting or coaching through Skype or Google Hangouts, creating and selling online courses, self-publishing eBooks, joining affiliate programs or selling physical products through an e-commerce store. There are unlimited possibilities, and we'll explore the most popular and rewarding ones.

***Here's an overview of the main online business models:***

1. ***Freelancing***: If you have a particular skill like copywriting, video editing, or web designing, you can offer your expertise and get hired through platforms like Upwork.com, Freelancer.com, Guru.com, or even through your website. The downside of freelancing is that even if you are location-independent (can work from home or anywhere), you're still trading your time for money. Unless the work you do is very highly paid and you don't need to work too many hours to generate sufficient income, you might not achieve the lifestyle freedom you're aiming for.

2. ***Online Consulting***: If you're a coach or have a certain type of expertise, you can sell online consulting services over the phone or via a system like Skype. Keep in mind, however, that the same thing is true for online consulting as for freelancing, you're directly trading your time for money. However, since private consulting is usually very well paid, you might not need many clients to live well. You 're going to be amazed at the number of

struggling single moms who are willing to learn how to turn their lives around.

3. ***Creating and Selling Your Own Digital Products***: This is usually the business model that generates the highest revenues. The most common products sold online include eBooks, audio tracks and online courses. You can sell them on your website, through other people's networks, or platforms like Gumroad.com.

4. ***Affiliate Marketing***: Affiliate marketing is a partnership between a business that has a product to sell and another business that agrees to promote that same product in exchange for a commission. Affiliate programs can be used in two ways:

Recommending other people's products to your audience and receiving a commission for each sale you make. This can work very well if you already have an audience that trusts you and you have built an email list.

Letting others sell your product, and offering them a commission for each sale they make. If you have the expertise or knowledge needed to create a good product, then creating such partnerships is an effective way to increase your sales, since you'll reach a larger audience. It's also a good method to expand your brand awareness.

Generally, affiliate commissions for digital products vary between 40% and 75%. Why such a high percentage? Because once created, digital products don't cost anything to reproduce. Thus, for the product initiator, this means generating extra sales at no extra cost. Affiliates can be a great way to generate a significant income. It's a very genuine form of advertising since you only recommend products that you sincerely believe your audience will benefit from.

5. ***Donation***: You could even ask your website visitors to give a voluntary donation. If you provide incredible value and have built an audience of real fans, they may agree to contribute to your site by donating. You simply have to add a donation button to your page that visitors can click on and enter their payment details. To help you set this system up, PayPal.com has a step-by-step guide for creating such a button. One blogger who has been using this method is Maria Popova, at BrainPickings.org.

6. ***Sponsored Articles***: If another entrepreneur shares the same target audience, but offers products or services that are complementary to yours (not in direct competition), he or she could write an article on your blog subtly

presenting his/her company or product. The other entrepreneur can pay you for the opportunity to expose his/her brand to your audience.

7. *Membership Websites*: In this case, the buyer (member) pays a recurring fee to have access to information, a product or service. One thing to consider with such a business model is that it requires you to constantly add new content to justify the recurring cost. I believe that it's easier to start by creating single products before considering launching a membership site, which is more work.

8. *Forums*: Most forums are free to access, but some are private and re□uire a fee to join. This business model is built around the value of being part of a community. Forums can take a significant amount of time to build and attract enough members to generate considerable income.

9. *Live Online Events*: These can be very lucrative. They can take the form of short webinars, usually one to three hours, or longer events that can last few days. These events are the online version of a workshop or an entire convention. They are less expensive to attend and to organize as they re□uire fewer logistics than traditional offline events. Their virtual nature also makes it easier for attendees and speakers from all around the world to participate. Webinars are typically free to attend and are used as an opportunity to introduce a premium (paid) product. They usually teach something useful, but at an incomplete level, so people are then encouraged to buy the paid service for a better result or to have access to all the relevant information. However, some webinars do require a fee to attend.

10. *Brokerage*: Brokers connect buyers to sellers and facilitate transactions. Some companies in this category are eBay, Priceline, Expedia, Amazon, PayPal, Craigslist, Airbnb, and Fiverr.com. Brokers are connectors. Choosing this type of business model means creating an exchange platform and receiving commissions for transactions or simply charging a fee to the seller and/or buyer.

11. *Sponsorship*: Sponsorship is a type of advertising in which one gives the money in exchange for exposure and visibility. For example, the most popular podcasters generate revenues for their show through sponsors. They mention the show sponsors during the episodes and give them increased visibility. This is also a business model that is often used with live events.

12. *Advertising*: Another business model involves renting advertising space on your website to businesses that have a specific message for your

audience. When you're just starting, the simplest way to do this is to use third-party advertising platforms. These serve as intermediaries between advertisers and site owners. As a site owner, you set up an account with the third-party ad platform, place ads on your website, and collect revenues based on ad impressions or clicks. The downside to this method is that you give up some revenue to the third-party service provider. The most common ad platform used for this method is Google AdSense. It's very easy to set up simply create an account and follow the directions. To maximize the effectiveness of this business model, you should choose to display contextual ads i.e. ads relevant to the topic of your site. You can select this option in your AdSense account. You could also sell ad space directly to businesses. This method will generate higher revenues since you don't need to share with an intermediary. However, you need a significant presence for this option and considerable traffic to attract advertisers. Advertising can be an interesting model if your site gets a lot of traffic. However, since it's rarely a sufficient source of income by itself, it's usually used as a complement to another business model.

To that end, this checklist describes what you need to do to begin wading into your own online business:

*Make the decision to commit*: You need to acknowledge that you're ready to pursue your goal. I do not doubt that you are going to commit as you have come this far

*Set clear goals*: Write down your expectations from this online business. These goals can be related to financial objectives, lifestyle goals, or both. If you know what you're looking for, you can also more easily choose the right business to meet your needs.

*Talk with your family*: After you commit to your idea and establish your goals, share your plan. Involve your kids and close relatives, you must talk about your vision for the future. After all, your dream for an online business affects that person's life too.

*Create an action timeline:* Unlike the broad goals, you set in the first item in this list, writing down specific action steps can help you realize tangible results. From researching business ideas to obtaining a business license, assign a targeted date of completion to further ensure that you make each step happen.

*Identify a business*: You can choose from different types of businesses to operate online. Before going any further, however, you have to decide which business to pursue. Narrow your choices by thinking about what you enjoy doing or which specific □ualifications you might already possess. Consider your professional experience and your desires. You might even have a hobby that can be developed into a moneymaking business.

*Develop your business idea:* Define your idea and determine how you will turn it into a profitable online business.

After you make it through this checklist, you're ready to go to work and transform your dream into a legitimate business. Internet is a world of its own, with different people seeking diverse products they can buy. The trick is the mind. I hope that starting an online business will bring you the joy and satisfaction that it has brought other single moms. You are the only one in the way of your success. **Since you're a single mother I already know that you have what it takes. You're a master at time management, you are responsible, and you work hard for everything you have. Now it's time you work hard to do something for YOU!**

# CHAPTER THREE

*STEP TWO: DEVELOP YOUR BUSINESS IDEA*

**M**any individuals want to start a business and become their bosses, but one of the main barriers that hold them back is their uncertainty regarding what business to start. Not knowing where to start, most people choose to stay in the environment they know, their current job. The most important and perhaps, most time-consuming step in creating your business is coming up with a viable, long term idea. When thinking about what you want to do there are several factors that you need to take into consideration. Your business idea should be something that interests you and will continue to hold your interest long term. The idea needs to have a specific market or niche (subject). And lastly, the idea needs to be profitable. I will help simplify the term with the analogy below;

A business idea usually results from this equation:

A topic you're interested in + People you like and want to help + A problem these people have + A solution you can provide to the problem, which you'll pack into a product or service in the format of your choice (book, video, course, etc.).

If you already have a business idea, you'll simply need to validate it. I'll discuss this aspect later in the book. That being said, if you haven't found an idea yet, this is the time to start ⬜uestioning yourself.

**The first step** is to reflect on your interests and the lifestyle you would like to attain, as well on your natural strengths and the skill set you already possess.

*What do you dislike about your current job and lifestyle? What would you like to change?*

There must be something, or even many things, that you dislike about your current situation. I believe that positive anger can be channelled into launching a new idea that birth your freedom. Maybe it's a lack of free time with your kids, your commute to work, being told what to do, the nature of the tasks you are re□uired to execute, or insufficient income.

It's important to define what you are trying to escape from so you avoid recreating it in your new lifestyle. For example, if a lack of time is a major issue, then you shouldn't opt for a business model that will re□uire an equal amount of your time (like freelancing, for example). Instead, you should choose a model that generates a passive income.

*What do you appreciate about your current situation and would like to maintain?*

Not everything is necessarily wrong with your current situation. Maybe you enjoy the relationships with your kids, close relatives and working in a team. You probably appreciate not having to think about work once you've clocked out. It's good to know what you like to reproduce it in your online business. For example, even if being a web entrepreneur mainly means working by yourself, there are ways to add social occasions to your new entrepreneurial life. You could attend training groups or conference for single moms or trailblazers in your field and occasionally meet with other like-minded entrepreneurs.

*What are your main interests?*

Some topics and activities are naturally more appealing to you than others. You feel more enthusiastic about certain conversation topics and are more curious to learn about some subjects. If you're planning on creating a blog or even if you aren't, think of a topic that you could write about every day, without growing bored or lacking inspiration.

*Answer the following □uestions:*

When you enter a bookstore, which section do you head to first?

Which kind of magazines do you read while waiting at the dentist?

Which TV channels do you watch?

Which sections of the newspaper do you like to read?

Which activities do you engage in during your free time?

Which websites do you like browsing?

It's important to choose a topic that you're interested in since it will become a part of your daily life. Otherwise, you will eventually get bored, sometimes sooner rather than later. It's important to note that, over time, you might discover that your interests are slightly different than what you initially thought. Sometimes, there are activities that you enjoy as a hobby, but not necessarily as a job.

You will be surprised that what you thought you love doing might not be fun and so boredom and tiredness is inevitable. I will recommend that you explore a topic you love and write it for a few weeks before choosing that subject for your business project. Without any limitation, Go out and try new activities, attend events or learn a new skill. Think of something you have always been curious about, and talk to people already engaged in that activity. Also, be curious about the people you meet. Ask them about their jobs, their interests, and their projects. It might be uncomfortable at first, but it will help you generate new ideas.

*Put that interest to test against time and do your research*

### What are your natural talents and strengths?

We're not talking about skills □uite yet. Natural talents and strengths are not necessarily abilities that you've gained through practice and experience; they are activities that naturally come easier for you than for others. You might be very good at writing and playing with words, performing manual tasks, solving problems, or analyzing concepts.

### What are your "natural" weaknesses?

Be careful not to think of weakness as a lack of skills, because skills can be learned. Your "natural" weaknesses are aspects with which you feel less at ease. For example, maybe you don't have a well-developed sense of aesthetics or struggle with organization. As a single mom, you should adopt a growth mindset and a desire to constantly work on your weaknesses to improve you, but it's still wise to acknowledge what comes naturally easy for you, so you don't pick a business model that will make things unnecessarily hard at the beginning.

### What's your personality like?

Certain aspects of your personality will determine which contexts will bring you more joy and fulfilment than others, in the same way, that your strengths and natural talents will.

### What are your skills, experience, and expertise?

Other elements to keep in mind are your skills and expertise. These are the abilities and knowledge that you have ac□uired overtime at work and through other activities. Starting your business around your current skills and expertise will help you move faster in the process since you won't have to spend too much time acquiring related knowledge. However, it's not mandatory to be an expert, nor even very experienced. **Don't forget that you can always learn**.

*To sell information products, you only need to know a little more than some people.*

### Find a niche topic.

Once you've found a topic that you're interested in. For example, photography, you'll need to get more specific as to which aspect of the topic you want to cover. We call this "niching down your topic."

A niche topic is a narrower category within your topic, such as outdoor photography, versus general photography. Choosing a niche topic versus a broader topic will increase the chances of your business being successful because the competition won't be as prevalent. Starting a business around a very broad topic is a common mistake made by new entrepreneurs. It's very difficult to compete for attention and market share with companies that are already well established. By choosing a narrower, more specific topic, you will increase your chances of standing out and getting noticed. You'll also build your authority in the field and generate revenues faster.

*A good example to illustrate this idea is this;*

Let's say that you're an online marketer interested in social media. There are already many well-established social media experts, which makes the sphere □uite competitive. Instead of trying to compete against well-known experts, you could choose another tactic. You could decide to become an expert in a newer social platform, like TikTok. Write about a different aspect of the platform every day for 60 days, at the end of that period, you could be seen as an "expert," in that niche since few people will have explored the same topic in such detail. Once you have established your authority and your credibility as an expert, you could choose to expand your field of expertise to other social media.

If you aren't sure which topic to pick, you could always consider one within these proven-to-be-profitable categories:

Health and well-being

Personal development

Dating

Business and finance

There will always be space to enter one of these topic markets since they correspond to needs that many people want to satisfy or common problems they wish to solve. You could easily choose a specific aspect (niche) within one of these broad categories. For example; losing pregnancy weight, dating for seniors, paying back student loans or overcoming a fear of public speaking.

Finally, to help you get through this introspection, and define what you want, a good exercise is to visualize your ideal day as a single mom, ideal week, and ideal year. Consider this: "If money wasn't a factor, how would I like to spend my days?" Then, try to find a way to generate an income that is close to that ideal.

***Lastly, take a look at businesses that others have started can help you develop your ideas.*** If you browse the Internet and search for topics you like and add the term "business" or even along with the topic in the search field, you'll almost certainly find examples of what others have done. For example, if you look for "fashion online business," you'll find many different types of online fashion businesses.

The inspiring stories of people who have successfully started all kinds of businesses are also great resources and are readily available by listening to podcasts. This can help you to consider many opportunities that you wouldn't have even thought of before. Podcasts are free to download from the iTunes store; some of the best business-related Podcasts include The School of Greatness, Entrepreneur on Fire, and The Smart Passive Income.

*Create Your Idea*

*Take some time to think about what business idea will best suit you. After you have narrowed down a few ideas, do some research and take a few days to really think about your options. It's important to choose the right idea the first time. You don't want to waste your valuable time working on an idea only to change it every few months.*

*Once you have your idea, it's time to get to know marketing a little better!*

# CHAPTER FOUR

*STEP THREE: CHOOSE YOUR NICHE MARKET: YOUR IDEAL CUSTOMERS*

As a single mother, I know that you have some built-up frustration and maybe even anger. You are already independent and maybe stressed most of the time. The great thing about starting an online business is it allows you to release stress. Your business is a positive and productive outlet. Single moms are some of the strongest people in the world and you've got what it takes to kill it when it comes to marketing. We've already mentioned the term niche which means "more specific" and the importance of choosing a niche topic for your business. When we say niche market versus niche topic, we are referring to the people to whom you're trying to sell your product, not to the product itself i.e. **your target market**.

You introduce your product or service to your target market. They are your potential audience, clients, or buyers.

Your market = Your audience (or potential clients or customers)

In marketing, we use the term mass markets and niche markets to describe how broad or specific the group of people we are trying to reach to sell our product or service is. A mass-market is very broad, meaning almost everyone, while a niche is narrow, representing a smaller group of people who share distinct characteristics.

These characteristics are usually related to demographic and psychographic traits, including interests, behavior, background and context, as well as the goal or end-result this target audience is trying to achieve. For example, let's consider two individuals looking to hire a fashion designer. One is a model who wants to go for a photo-shoot, and the other is a bride who needs a wedding dress for her wedding. Both are looking for a professional fashion designer, but for very different reasons. Not only do these two individuals belong to distinctive demographic groups, but they are also driven by different motives. They should be considered as comprising two different market niches. Thus, within broad markets, you can find many sub-markets or niches.

*"You are not creating products or services for everyone. You are creating them for the discerning ones, the ones with the particular needs or tastes you can satisfy, or the very specialist problems you can solve." - Mark McGuiness,*

That's exactly what the concept of a niche is targeting the people predisposed to being pleased by what you have to offer, and excluding all others in your marketing efforts.

### Know Your Target Market before Creating a Product

To increase the probability of your business's success, choosing a market should come before creating a product.

To avoid the mistakes of other businesses. Do not create a product blindly and then attempt to push it into the market through advertising and trying to persuade people to buy it. This method often fails. The more efficient way to build a business is to choose a market first, and find out what the needs of that specific market are, before creating customized products in response to those needs.

This is much more effective when you follow this se□uence:

Choose a market.

Find the needs of that market.

Create products that solve the market's problems (needs).

### Choose a Niche Market

It's usually best not to "pitch" to everyone. However, that does raise the □uestion of how narrow your market should be. Generally, for an online business, you have the advantage of being as narrow as possible (by "possible," I mean as long as you have a large enough potential client pool within your niche to have a profitable business).

But remember, the Internet is a very large pool! The number of potential customers isn't limited by location, as it is for an offline business. Thus, you can easily have sufficient customers online, even within a very specific market.

Also, you don't have to feel "stuck" with your niche choice. After choosing your niche, you aren't immediately stuck with your choice forever you can expand your reach later. Once you are well established within your niche and have developed a reputation, you can expand more easily.

Here's an example: A friend of mine, Angelina, is interested in creating swimwear for women. Since there are already many established brands in the industry, she could choose to cater to a specific market, such as women with very small breast size. She could create swimsuits specifically designed for their shape to make that "niche" of customers look their best and feel more confident.

Eventually, once she's well established in her market, she could decide to expand and target women with very large breast size, for example, and create a completely different line of swimsuits perfectly designed for the needs of that target clientele. Angelina could keep expanding her product lines this way by focusing on being great at serving one segment (niche) at a time.

### Reasons why you should choose a Niche?

1. You'll have a better chance of standing out and getting noticed, and you will gain authority in your field faster. It's difficult to enter a market and compete against leaders who are already well known for their work in a given field. However, if you focus on one specific aspect or niche and explore it, there is a good chance that you'll become more knowledgeable than most people and will be considered the go-to person in that specific market.

2. You'll make more sales. People are looking for a specific answer to a specific problem, so they prefer to buy something that corresponds to their precise needs. They buy the "best match" possible, because they believe it will help them solve their problem the best. If you've addressed your marketing message to a specific group of people, they are more likely to feel engaged and feel that their needs are understood, and ultimately buy what you are selling.

Mara Tyler is a copywriting expert. She helps website owners perfect their message in their writing. On her website, she mentions that she mainly works with coaches and people operating in fields related to health and personal development. These are the clients she prefers and has the most experience working with. As a personal coach, that needed help with the copywriting, I would rather re␣uest the service of Mara Tyler than go for another copywriter who works with any kind of website that hires her. Furthermore, I believe she would correspond better to my specific needs, which might probably lead to a willingness to pay a higher fee for her services.

3. You'll enjoy your work more because you get to choose your niche. By picking a niche, you get to choose the people who you'll work with and eliminate the ones you would prefer to avoid. In short, you'll be happier.

4. You'll handle your marketing easily. Reaching a mass-market (everyone) is hard work and re␣uires a lot of money which are not necessarily effective. When you select a specific type of people (niche) to offer a product or a service, it's easier and faster to find where these people "hang out" (both online and offline) and find effective ways to reach them.

For example, different groups of people with distinctive objectives will use different social media platforms. Depending on the psychographic and demographic features of your market, you'll be able to determine which platform your target market uses the most. These are the platforms where you should expose your brand.

Many marketing sites, such as Pew Research Center, published studies on social media users that you can use to determine where you'll have a better chance of reaching your audience. Your topic will also determine which platform to favor. If your product is very visual, like photography, paintings, or crafts, platforms like Instagram and Pinterest work very well to transmit your message and connect with your audience.

***There are three main aspects to keep in mind when selecting a niche:***

1. Choose a niche you are interested in serving.

2. Make sure it's profitable. You also need to make sure that your niche is profitable by considering the following factors;

Affordability; For example, a single parent on social benefits probably won't have the money to buy expensive unessential goods. Is your product or service affordable? Or are your customers willing to spend money on your product or service?

Competition; the easiest way when you are just starting is by looking at the competition. Are there successful businesses already serving the same market? If so, that means there are enough buyers. Competition is usually a good sign.

Empathy; you need empathy to connect with your potential customers to build trust with them and be able to sell them your product or service. Your target audience should, therefore, be a past or a present version of yourself, or at least people who you understand very well, have a deep interest in serving, and can easily have access to so you can gather helpful information about their needs and desires.

Validate; However, it's important to mention that you should always research to validate what you think you know about your niche. Even if your audience is a past or a present version of yourself and represents the people you think you know well, always do your research to confirm and back up what you think with real data because you could be wrong.

In this information era, there is no need to guess. Today, with the Internet, you can research and find real data. A rookie mistake is to make assumptions. You can research popular topics and business trends on these websites: Magazines.com, Ezinearticles.com, Amazon.com, Clickbank.com, and FindaForum.net.

If for some reason you still don't see the need for or advantage of targeting a narrower market to sell your products, or if you have a portfolio of products that you want to sell to different types of people, remember that, at the very least, your message itself must be formulated differently for different target markets.

### Dealing with Criticism

It's essential to take criticism with a growth mindset, meaning that you should see every challenge as an opportunity to grow. Having a growth mindset means using all constructive criticism as feedback, and regarding it as an opportunity to learn and improve. Notice that I said constructive criticism. That's the only negative feedback you should bother to listen to and be concerned about. Unhelpful comments with the sole intention of hurting shouldn't get even a slight bit of your attention, they aren't worth it.

*Find Your Niche Market And Have A Growth Mindset.*

*Think about who your ideal customer is. Make a list of all the places your ideal client would be. Try "thinking outside the box." Can you find your audience on and offline? What do your audience like to do? What problem can you help them with?*

34

# CHAPTER FIVE

CREATE YOUR IDEAL CUSTOMER'S AVATAR PROFILE

The best way to do this is by creating the most realistic version of one, two, or even three different members of your ideal audience. And yes, to create such a profile, you should use real data. This process should be taken very seriously because it can have a tremendous impact on the overall success of your business. You can give your business a much better chance of success by investing time upfront getting to know the audience, understanding their problems, their language, and their values so the chances of creating a successful business for that audience are much higher.

The key is: get the right head, heart, and data about your audience and make something valuable for them!"

### How to Create Your Ideal Customer's Avatar Profile

First, I'd like to point out the emphasis on the term ideal. I want you to work with customers who are interesting to you and exclude others. That's why we'll create those ideal customers' profiles these are the customers you'll try to reach.

This profile contains; Demographic Description, Age, Gender, Location, Occupation, Marital status and family situation, Psychographic Description (i.e. Lifestyle, Values, Priorities), Hobbies Behavior and attitude, and Goals and Motivation.

The more information you can gather, the better. Knowing your ideal customers will make it easier for you to find out where they "hang out." Once you know the appropriate platform to reach your audience, you'll be able to listen to the conversations they are having and communicate with them more effectively. Detecting and understanding their problems, goals, and motivations, makes you better suited to create the best solution (product) for them.

That's how you'll make more sales. Obviously, the customers' avatars that you will create won't represent all members of your audience perfectly, but you should be aware of and look for commonalities among the members of your niche.


### *Where Do You Find Information About Your Ideal Customer?*

The first rule is to never assume. You'll have to do some research. The research will differ if you already have an audience (past or current customers, clients, or blog readers) versus if you are starting from scratch. However, even if you don't have an existing audience, you can find valuable information online and offline after just a few hours of research.

*Some tricks you can use to enhance your research:*

1. Interview someone you know whose profile aligns with your target audience

2. Meet new people by creating groups or join already available groups that have your target audience. You can reach out via social media platforms

3. Ask people who work or deal with your target market.

4. Go to FindAForum.net and search for one related to your niche.

5. Find popular blogs in your niche to get an idea on your tone in relating with your target audience

6. Use surveys to ask □uestions. Even if you don't already have an audience, you could survey people representing your niche market, depending on the context. The survey should be short. Think of the most useful information you'd like to obtain.

Another platform you can explore include Quora, Facebook ads and Google analytics.

## MARKETING IS EMPATHY

One of the most important aspects of marketing is empathy. You gain customers, clients, or readers once you have been able to put yourself in their shoes and speak their language. You make sales after you have built connections and trust. That's exactly what empathy will help you do. Once you have defined your ideal customers' profiles, you should take a few minutes to create an empathy map i.e. the average day of your target audience, their likes and dislikes.

In 80/20 Sales and Marketing, Perry Marshall writes "One of the cardinal rules of marketing is to never go into a market unless you can write a page of your customers' diary and be so spooky-accurate that they wonder: 'Hey, were you spying on me last night?' That way, you won't make the mistake of jumping into a swimming pool that has no water in it. Don't try to sell something that nobody wants to buy."

While planning to create products or services for your market, you absolutely need to put yourself in your customers' shoes and see life from their perspective in order to accurately create solutions they will want to buy.

That's the main reason you have spent so much effort defining your niche market and why you have chosen one that you know and/or have a deep interest in serving. It's also why you've spent time defining the profile (avatar) of this niche.

Knowing your audience and its daily reality is crucial for every aspect of your business. It will reflect in the copy of your website, primarily in the about page, homepage, blog posts, and sales pages. Although they say that an email list is an organization's most important asset, it's the relationship that you nurture with the subscribers to your list that is even more valuable. To build those strong relationships, you need to demonstrate empathy. Then, and only then, will the subscribers like you, trust you, and buy from you.

# CHAPTER SIX

*STEP FIVE: BRANDING*
YOUR BRAND IS YOUR IDENTITY.

Your brand represents how you want the world to see you, and also how the world sees you. In fact, good branding is located at the intersection of these two perspectives, and brand management works to keep a company in that zone.

Your identity is a mixture of tangible and intangible elements, which, altogether, contribute to creating a mental image of your organization in consumers' minds. It is your job to make sure the world sees the real you, and that this mental representation of your business is close to the image you want to project.

Your brand should differentiate you from your competitors in your field and it should also determine who your buyers will be. Some consumers will choose you over other options on the market because of your remarkable offer and because they have connected with your brand, most likely on an emotional level.

Simon Sinek demonstrates in his book that great organizations are those built on a strong purpose. He states that "people don't buy what you do, they buy 'why' you do it."

The question you ask when branding is "**THE WHY**" i.e. Why do you want to create a line of swimwear? A travel blog? A consulting business? A yoga course?

A real purpose is more profound than simply generating an income. Of course, the reason behind every business is to generate a profit, but the purpose behind why you started the business itself goes far beyond that.

Good branding is no longer optional. In fact, 48% of consumers report that they are more likely to become loyal to a brand during the first purchase or experience.

### Define your core values

Defining your core values is an important step forward. It's not just about describing your business, it's about giving you a guideline to follow. It will help you decide which projects to take, which collaborators to work with, and which future employees to hire because all these decisions should be made in line with your core values.

**Your core values become your company's culture code**. They guide your decisions and determine the kind of people you'll connect and build relationships with. They also determine who will be interested in doing business with you.

### Mission and Vision Statements

Your mission statement is a one-or two-sentence explanation of what your business is about and its reason for existing. Your mission statement should be inspirational. As Richard Branson, founder of the Virgin Group, says: "Brevity is certainly key, so try using Twitter's 140-character template when you're drafting your inspirational message."

*You need to explain your company's purpose and outline expectations for internal and external clients alike. Make it uni□ue to your company, make it memorable, and keep it real."*

A mission statement should be general enough to stay relevant for several years but still contain enough information to understand the core purpose, personality, and offerings of a company. It should become a fundamental guide for your daily actions. This information is usually found in the about section of a company's website. You can check various about section of any website to have an idea. Amazon.com mission statement reads "To be Earth's most customer-centric company where people can find and discover anything they want to buy online."

Your vision is the roadmap for your business's future. Vision is like the larger goal or dream behind your business, the optimal desired future state.

Through your vision, you can express your ideas and what you wish to accomplish on a larger scale than just within your organization.

The bottom line is that who you are in business should be a reflection of who you are in your personal life. Defining your values, purpose, and what you stand for, as well as remaining true to them, will inspire trust and respect from your audience.

### *Beat The Competition*

It's hard to become the best player in a given field because the title of "best" is subjective and difficult to evaluate. Furthermore, engaging in such a competitive approach is like getting into a rat race, there will always be other players trying to beat you at your own game. This kind of endless race is energy-consuming, and unless you have unlimited marketing and advertising funds, it's not a viable approach. Therefore, it would be smarter and more effective to capitalize on something else: your uniqueness. No one has the same background and experience and story as yours. The combination of your story, values, mission, perspective, and what you stand for is unique. This is the one place where you are sure to win; no one can beat you at being yourself.

It might sound a little cheesy, but I believe it should also be a relief to know that all you have to do is take some time to be introspective and answer a few questions about yourself, and about what you want to share with the world to correctly define your identity, your brand.

### *Own and Tell Your Story*

A great way to differentiate your brand is through a story, own your story! Think of a fun anecdote about the creation of your business when you first stumbled upon the idea. Talk about your challenges and struggles of being a single mom or relative issues depending on your audience.

These stories can be related to important people, places, events or things in our lives. For example, a first date, a memorable vacation or a childhood family home might all fit within this collection. Write down and collect those stories to eventually use them by creating analogies to illustrate ideas. Stories are a great way to develop a connection. They humanize your business and allow people to bond with you and your ideas more easily. They raise the connection with your audience to an emotional level.

### *Your Unique Selling Proposition (USP)*

Your unique selling proposition (USP) is how you do what you do in a way that is different from the other players in your field. It's how you differentiate yourself from your competitors. It's your unique, competitive advantage, the benefit only you can offer. Basically, your USP should be formulated in a very clear message that explains your offer (product or service), and why it should be chosen over the other options available on the market. To achieve this, the proposition must be remarkable and must promise outstanding value.

A Business coach can specialize in coaching artists, such as actors, writers, and musicians. His USP clearly states that his/her expertise is directed towards helping individuals operating in creative fields to build their creative business or take it to the next level.

Note that, it's not smart to compete on the same stage as the big players, especially not when you're just starting and have zero audiences, credibility, and authority. The only way you can get noticed is by not doing the same thing as everyone else!

### *Proper positioning of your product*

Positioning your product well is just as important as the product itself. It determines how it will be received by the market, and therefore determines its success. Your goal should be to get the right people to purchase your product, rather than just selling as many of your products as possible. Positioning is simply an effort to influence consumer perception of a brand or product relative to the perception of competing brands or products. Its objective is to occupy a clear, uni□ue, and advantageous position in the consumer's mind."

Positioning is how you are compared to your competitors in consumers' minds. It's your uni□ue selling proposition in comparison to those of other players. The difference between your USP and positioning is that positioning is based completely on the consumers' perceptions, it's the image of your organization or product from their perspective.

For example, a wrong positioning can lead to a product's failure, think of an online course for learning the Russian language. If the course is designed at an intermediate level and focuses on the advanced level, this should be explicitly mentioned in the course description. This is because a true beginner learning the language and planning a trip to Russia might be disappointed by what the course delivers. The product would simply not be appropriate for this learner's needs.

Finally, before defining the position you would like to ac□uire in the market, take a look at your competitors and at what has already been done. This will help you to have a better idea of where to position your brand.

## THE ELEMENTS THAT SUPPORT YOUR ESSENCE
### Your Organization and Product or Service Name
The name of your organization does matter. It should be simple to understand, to spell, to remember, and to associate with your offer. Ideally, it should easily create a mental image of what you are all about in your consumers' mind, the right image.

### Your Visual Identity
You need to choose your visual identity carefully because it's not something you will change much over time. This visual representation of your brand has to be consistent on all platforms, in social media, and other promotional material.

### Colors and Fonts
In branding, consistency is a basic rule to respect. You don't want to create confusion in your consumer's mind. You want to build a strong brand and visual elements which are a crucial component of the image associated with your organization. This means that the colors and fonts you decide to use to create your visual identity should be consistent.

Certain colors evoke certain emotions and perceptions and are associated with certain types of businesses and fields. For example, if you offer gardening services, it would be natural to choose green tones, but not as many purple tones. Purple is often associated with alternative medicines. Blue is a color of trust and professionalism, whereas orange often relates to creativity.

Depending on the type of business you have, the field you operate in, and how you want people to perceive you, you'll choose a certain color palette to support your branding efforts.

The fonts you use should also reinforce the identity of your business. For example, a law firm wouldn't look very professional using a typographical script style on its website.

43

## Logo

As with a name, a logo must be simple and easily recognizable. It should be uni☐ue, as it's an important element used to differentiate yourself from other players. Your logo is an important part of your branding. It will appear on your promotional material, on your business cards, on your website, in your email signature, etc. It's like a signature in itself. A properly drawn vector design will provide you with the ultimate flexibility to use your logo in different ways and different sizes. **You only get one chance for a first impression, so make it a good one.**

## Create a strong online presence; Website

An online presence for a business is the business's website, social profiles, online memberships in directories, and any other places on the Internet where customers and potential customers can find you. It's the collective sum of all identities you've created on the Internet.

The simple act of creating a website will make your business more appealing and trustworthy to a wide group of consumers. About 56% of consumers don't trust a business that doesn't have a website. Think about that for a moment. More than half of consumers won't trust your business if it doesn't have an online presence. Consumers who don't trust your business are unlikely to become customers. A website is a critical first step in establishing your online presence.

## The tone of communication

Another subtler component of branding is your tone of voice. Your tone of voice is the way you communicate your message and the language you use through different platforms and channels. It's closely related to the personality of your brand, to your core values, and your chosen approach.

If you offer consulting services, sell online courses or host workshops, your tone will primarily be educational. You'll use proper, respectful, and an easy-to-understand language to make sure your audience gets your message. If you write a travel blog and mainly tell anecdotes, maybe you'll choose a more casual or even humorous tone. You have to decide: if you want to be more formal or chatty, serious or funny, detached or warm, opinionated or neutral.

As a brand component, your voice should be aligned with your values, mission, vision, and all the other elements that contribute to creating the correct image for your organization, which is the image you want to produce in your consumer's mind.

### *Elevator Pitch*

You should be able to Express Your Brand. Introduce who you are and what you do in a way that quickly captures your audience's interest and makes them sufficiently intrigued to want to know more about your "cause" (your idea, project, organization or product) in 40 seconds. Every pitch is focused on inspiring interest in others about what you have to offer. Avoid jargon and expert terms; instead, communicate your message using wording that is easy to understand. Metaphors are also a great way to help people remember your brand. For example, "Our swimwear is so comfortable, it feels like a second skin."

### *Here's an elevator pitch example for a swimwear designer:*

"We help women feel glamorous and comfortable in their skin (intrigue). We design uni☐ue pieces of swimwear for women that perfectly fit with their body type, and enhance their features. We believe that every woman should feel beautiful. Our swimwear is elegant and also adapted to an active lifestyle. It allows comfort and ease of movement. All our swimwear is made locally with environmentally-friendly methods and materials. When you buy our product, you also contribute to an environmental cause, since 10% of the profits go to a water preservation organization. Our swimwear can be found online.

### *The Rules to Respect in Branding*

1. *Alignment*: you should align your branding efforts. Your message (tone) should be aligned with your values and purpose. The same goes for your visual identity, which should also be chosen based on the nature of your organization and offering (product or service type). Congruence is key. It's almost impossible to inspire trust if all the elements that compose your brand aren't aligned. Your business would look "sketchy."

2. *Clarity*: It's also your job to make sure that the message you send to your target market is crystal clear so that your offer is well understood. As they say, a confused mind doesn't buy. Use simple language, not industry language that the average consumer won't understand. Don't hide details about your offer.

3. **Consistency**: Remember to be consistent with the tone of your communication and in the visual aspect of your brand (colors, fonts, logo, and design). You want people to easily recognize your organization.

### Brand Monitoring

To stay on the lookout for what's being said about your brand, tools like Google Alerts allow you to receive updates when your brand is mentioned on the Internet. You can use the same tool to monitor what's being said about your competitors. Also, pay attention to the comments your audience makes about you on social media, in the comment section of your blog, or elsewhere.

*"There are no secrets to success. It is the result of preparation, hard work, and learning from failure."* – Colin Powell

# CHAPTER SEVEN

*STEP SIX: THE TECHNICAL ASPECTS*

The technical part of an online business isn't really an element of the blueprint, it's not a determinant of your success but as it is a major concern for many aspiring online single mom, I felt that we had to explore this aspect, as well.

If you're comfortable with technology, building your website and adding plugins (pieces of software code), then this won't be difficult for you at all. However, for less tech-savvy single moms, technology can be stressful, at least until you begin to understand how it works.

As a single mother, you are already the queen of time management. You may be reluctant to try and s□ueeze more time from your day, but in the end, you will be glad you did. Your new business is going to re□uire at least two hours of your time every day to be successful. After your business takes off you may be able to spend a little less time on it. Or, you may want to spend more time to maximize your profit potential.

You may fall in love with the work that comes along with this new business and spends more time on it than you ever imagined! It's very rewarding to know that you have started an online business all by yourself, but more rewarding when you love what you do!

Now, if the Internet (or even computers themselves) makes you nervous, just take a deep breath, you'll see that it's not too complicated. I'm not a tech-savvy person, and I still manage to enjoy the technical part of my business.

CHOOSING A PLATFORM

There are two main options when building a website: self-hosted or not self-hosted.

To be found on the Web, your website must be "hosted" on a server. Web hosting is a service provided by a company that enables your website to be seen online. It's a bit like the online version of renting a physical space in a shopping center, so your store can be visited by potential buyers.

### Hosted platform

You could choose to build your site on a hosted platform, such as WordPress.com (different from WordPress.org), Weebly.com, SquareSpace.com, RainMakerPlatform.com (high-end option)

These platforms manage the software, data and web hosting for you, they even host your website content on their web server. This is a simpler option, and often an appropriate one for a "display" type of website. However, as you continue building your business, the functions will be too limited for your needs in the long run. You would need better SEO capabilities and other special features to help you grow your business.

### Self-hosted platform

You should use the content management system, WordPress.org (different from WordPress. com). This option includes registering a domain name, purchasing a web hosting plan and connecting them to WordPress.org.

### Below are steps to take;

1. Choosing a Domain Name: You'll need to purchase a domain for your new website, which usually costs around $10/year. You can purchase it directly with your web hosting provider. This will be less confusing. In most cases, it's better to use ".com" than any other domain endings such as .org, .co, or .ca. Also, choose one that doesn't confuse your brand with another's, and ideally use a ".com" ending.

2. Web hosting service: You'll also need a web hosting service, for which you can expect to pay around $5-$10/month. It's very important to select a reliable service, and I recommend BlueHost.com or HostGator.com. They both have 99.9% uptime (time your site is running) and provide excellent customer service.

### WordPress.org

WordPress.org is a content management system. It's the most commonly used platform for blogs and other websites. You do not need to know HTML coding to use it. It is a very flexible platform that you can customize in almost infinite ways. Many different plugins can also be added to a WordPress website. Plugins are pieces of software code that you install on your website to add new features and functions, a shopping cart, social media sharing buttons, a comment box, etc.

Once your WordPress account is created, I recommend watching the free tutorial videos from WpBeginner.com, which explain the different functions inside WordPress. Simply go to the video section of their website and register for access to the WordPress 101 series. You can also find many other free tutorials on YouTube.

### Installing plugins

To customize your website and add features, you can install numerous pieces of uni□ue software code, called plugins. On the left sidebar of your WordPress dashboard, click on "Plugins" and "Add New." You can use the search box to find different plugins by name.

### Stay calm

If you still don't feel comfortable registering your domain, getting a self-hosting plan, and setting up WordPress, don't get discouraged and don't spend hours trying to figure everything out, just go get help!

You do not have to do everything yourself. You can easily find someone you know or hire a specialist to do it for you. You could also take a course to learn more about WordPress. Udemy.com, Lynda.com, and SkillShare.com offer several paid online courses on the topic. You can also find an expert in your city if you prefer to meet in person—look on Craigslist or search on Google. It is also possible to outsource the entire process, or part of it, to a specialist for a fairly low cost. You can hire a freelancer on Fiverr.com, Freelancer.com or Upwork.com.

Just remember, don't get overwhelmed with the technical aspects of your online business. Everyone has started somewhere. You only have to be willing to learn. Furthermore, once you understand the technicalities, it isn't all that complicated!

*To help you create your website, here are important things to keep in mind;*

1. Keep the design simple, fresh and uni□ue. Again, your website reflects your brand. It is the first impression a visitor will form when they visit your site for the first time. If you use an off-the-shelf template and your website looks like thousands of other sites on the Internet, you'll miss an opportunity to create a unique impression. Consider the impression you want to make and the message that you want to communicate with your customers and potential

customers. Resist the urge to overload your homepage with a lot of text and images.

2. Showcase your products and services. Make sure that you showcase that product or service on your homepage. As mentioned earlier, you have only a few seconds to make a first impression and it has to be professional. If you're selling products and your customers will buy the products online, you need to make sure that the product photos or graphical images and descriptions are clean, crisp and appropriate.

3. Pay attention to site load times. People are impatient when browsing websites and slow load times impact conversions (getting people to buy your products or services). You can improve your site load times by picking good hosts. The cheapest monthly hosting option does not typically offer the best value.

4. Make your site easily accessible. Consider how people with certain disabilities (such as color blindness) can learn about your products and services if they visit your site. Also, consider how people with slower internet connections will view your site. This is especially important for small businesses, including rural small businesses, catering to local clients – accessibility is one of the best ways to endear your business to such clients.

5. Organize your site to provide a better user experience. Search engines prefer websites that are properly organized. People also prefer good organization. Keep in mind that when your prospective customers visit your site, they're typically looking for specific information. They're rarely going to read entire pages, they'll skim headlines and small portions of text and look at photos or graphics (but not all of them on the same page) thus, **the need for a good tagline**.

6. Content is important. The more content on your site, the more attractive your site becomes for search engines. Poor content can □uickly cause a visitor to leave your site. Keep the content fresh and current. Study your successful competitors especially those that have been in business longer than you. Look at their websites and study how they present their products and services to their customers and potential customers. But ensure you are unique.

*"Whatever the mind of man can conceive and believe, it can achieve. Thoughts are things! And powerful things at that, when mixed with*

*definiteness of purpose, and burning desire, can be translated into riches."* –
*Napoleon Hill*

# CHAPTER EIGHT

*STEP SEVEN: CREATE YOUR EMAIL LIST*

B uilding an email list for your business must be your number one priority, especially when you are just starting. Think of the 80/20 principle, 20 per cent of your effort brings 80 per cent of the benefits. Building your email list is the action that can lead to that 80 per cent.

As a Mompreneur, start building your email list sooner. You should start collecting emails as soon as your website has been created by offering a form where visitors can sign up. Using email marketing is an essential part of marketing that has proven to have the highest sales conversion rate. It permits you to relate with your target audience.

***Online business's Number One Asset***

An organization's email list is its number one asset or, more specifically, the relationship that a business has with its subscribers is its number one asset. The real assets are your engaged email subscribers, the ones interested in buying the product or service you offer.

Some marketers would argue that you are better off with a big list, and I don't disagree with them. However, what I am saying is that you're better off with a smaller list of high-□uality subscribers than a huge list of people uninterested in your offer. Of course, a bigger list of □uality subscribers is even better!

Direct email is a personal way to communicate with your audience members, to build rapport, and to maintain your relationship with them. Also, the most effective way to get accurate information about your audience; their needs, pains, and desires is by surveying them, which can easily be done through email. Questioning your subscribers is a great way to find out which product or service to eventually offer.

By contacting your email subscribers regularly, you also remind them of your existence. You can send them a notification when you publish a new article and encourage them to visit your blog. You can let them know about your new product, and send them promotions.

Emails are a free promotional channel through which you can reach the most targeted potential customers you could want: people who have already demonstrated an interest in your business. Not only is it a free means of advertising your product, but email marketing also has the highest sales conversion rate of any other promotional channel. An email list helps to create partnerships i.e. connect with other influencers in your industry.

*HOW TO BUILD YOUR EMAIL LIST*

The process of collecting email addresses is □uite simple. You need to have an opt-in form on your website for visitors to enter their information and an email marketing service to collect, store, and organize those email addresses.

Since people are reluctant to give away their personal information, you must provide them with a good reason to do so. In exchange for an email, you should offer a gift, which we call a lead magnet. Let's explore these elements in more detail.

### Email Marketing Service Provider

An email marketing service will provide a complete system to collect email addresses and organize them, create and automate the messages, and split test and track your campaigns. Most services charge a monthly fee, which usually depends on the number of subscribers you have the cost will increase as your list grows.

Elements to consider while choosing an email management provider include;

Automation: Make sure you can automate your messages by setting a pre-determined day and time when your emails are sent to your subscribers.

Segmentation: It's much better to segment people in your list according to their preferences and interests to increase the efficiency of your email campaigns. For example, you could separate people who have subscribed (and received a free eBook on exercising for weight loss) from the people who have signed up for a free Skype consultation for nutrition coaching. You can then create different email campaigns for each segment and send them offers that better correspond to their specific needs and interests.

A/B testing: Testing to improve your marketing tactics is a key determinant of your business's success. A/B testing means that you send one email version (A) to half of your subscribers, and a different version (B) to the other half, and observe which version converts best. Testing is how you optimize your email campaign and increase its results.

There are many email marketing service providers of varying complexity and price. Here are three that I recommend when you are just starting:

**AWeber.com**

Many marketers and business owners use AWeber since it's affordable. Its features include email automation, email marketing tracking, and subscriber segmentation.

**MailChimp.com**

MailChimp is another popular and easy-to-use email marketing service. Their free plan for up to 2,000 subscribers is interesting for entrepreneurs who are just starting. While the free plan only includes some basic features, you could consider beginning with this option and then upgrading later as the business grows.

**GetResponse.com**

GetResponse gives you access to all the features you need when you're starting your business. Their interface is very easy to navigate, and their video tutorials are simple to understand.

However, all of the email marketing systems mentioned above, and many others available on the market, can be good options. The trick is you can even try them all using their free trials and then decide which one you prefer.

*THE LEAD MAGNET*

For a freebie to be perceived as highly valuable, it must be something your audience really wants or even better, needs. Your freebie should be something that provides a solution to those issues in the same way that your paid product would. A high-value offer doesn't mean that it has to be costly and time-consuming to produce. It simply has to solve the problem.

For example, let's say you're a fitness trainer and sell online training programs for women wishing to have summer shaped body. Your freebie could be a cheat sheet of the five most effective exercises to build the necessary muscles. Would that be useful enough information to land an email address? Of course!

To increase its perceived value, the cheat sheet could be presented in a well-designed PDF, with images to demonstrate the exercises.

A lead magnet can take any of these forms namely; eBook, audio track, video, short course, checklist or cheat sheet, free Skype consultation. The freebie could be delivered all at once, or in an email series. A series could be, for example, a short video course in three parts.

An important element to consider when deciding on a freebie is that it has to be relevant to your paid product. Remember, your email subscribers are only valuable to you if they are potential customers or brand advocates.

In our previous example with the fitness trainer, the exercise cheat sheet was highly relevant to the paid product, the online fitness training programs. However, let's say the trainer thought of offering a video game as an opt-in incentive. That's not at all relevant. There is no reason to believe that the person opting-in for the video game would be interested in later purchasing fitness training. The two products aren't related.

### Opt-in Form

The opt-in form is the actual form through which visitors sign up by entering their information (usually their name and email). Opt-in forms can be placed in several strategic locations on your web page to optimize the number of visitors who sign up.

Your email marketing service should provide several form templates you can easily edit and customize. It's important to choose a form that matches your brand's design and looks clean and professional.

### The Text in the Form

The headline in the form should state the solution you offer and mention the freebie. Tell the visitors what they'll get after they sign up. Just under the headline, include some details about the freebie. It's a good idea to use bullet points.

For example, a headline could be "5 quick exercises to have a summer body." Then, give some details about the benefits, but keep it short. The message should be easily understandable at a glance. Use large fonts and colors that match your brand, but which also stand out on the web page.

### The Call-to-Action Button

The call-to-action button of the opt-in form also plays a role in the conversion. It is there to tell visitors what to do next. It's better to avoid using the boring and suspicion-inducing "Subscribe," and opt for a more benefit-oriented action verb, such as "Download Now" or "Get Instant Access." You'll also get better results by making the button stand out. Choose a contrasting color that attracts attention.

### The Sign-up Forms on Your Website

Little details, such as where you place the sign-up form on your web page, can lead to a huge difference in conversion in online marketing,

There are strategic places where you should place the forms on your website to increase your chances of converting visitors into subscribers.

1. *Above the fold*; this is the portion of the webpage that the visitors see when they arrive on your site, without having to scroll down.

2. *In the upper-right sidebar*; this is probably the most commonplace to insert an opt-in form— at the top of your right sidebar.

3. *Above the top menu*; there is a free plugin you can install within WordPress called Hello Bar that provides a thin, horizontal form just above your website's top navigation menu.

4. *After each blog post*; a person who has read one of your articles to the bottom has demonstrated a high interest in your content. That's the type of person you want to join your email list, and you should make it easy for him/her to do so by placing an opt-in form right after the post. You will get even better results if you offer a freebie that is relevant to the post topic.

5. *At the beginning of each post*; a tactic that also converts well, especially if you write long blog articles, is to give readers the possibility of downloading the PDF version of the article, which they can print or save to read later. The readers simply have to enter their email addresses to download the PDF.

6. *Pop-up forms*; the (sometimes annoying) pop-up sign-up forms actually convert better than almost anything else. Simply choose to use them on a few

pages that get most of your traffic. There are several types of pop-up form software available, and three good ones are PopUpDomination.com, ThriveThemes.com/leads and OptinMonster.com.

### CREATING A VALUABLE EMAIL CONTENT

The content of your emails must be valuable enough to make your subscribers want to open and read them. Thus, you must always provide useful information and should vary the content of your messages to keep them interesting.

Some examples of what you could send to your list include;

Useful resource or tool that you have consumed which you believe can help your customers achieve their goals,

Share a lesson you've learned to help your audience avoid making the same mistake

Tell a fun fact or story

Ask them a ◻uestion to engage them

Announce a promotion or discount on any of your products or services

Sell a product (your own or an affiliate's)

### Use conversational tone

Never forget what your email subscribers are real people. Craft your messages as if you were sending them to your friends. Use a conversational tone, and demonstrate a genuine desire to help. Most email marketing services will allow you to personalize your messages by automatically adding the real name of every subscriber. This is why you're often asked to enter your name along with your email address when filling in a sign-up form. Simple details like this will make your communication more personal. You can tell your subscribers not to hesitate to reply to your messages and to contact you if they have any ◻uestions. If you offer this, try to reply to every message. This will be easier to do while your list is small.

*Now that you have a whole system in place to build, nurture, and grow your business's main asset, your email list. There is only one thing that you're missing: traffic to your website.*

# CHAPTER NINE

*STEP EIGHT: GENERATE TRAFFIC TO YOUR WEBSITE*

A common analogy in online business is that, without traffic (visitors coming to your site), your website is like a billboard in the middle of the desert. Even if you write the most interesting posts, create the best products, or offer an outstanding service, if no one knows about it, your business won't get very far.

Driving traffic to your new business website can often seem like the biggest roadblock of your online business journey as a single mom but just like every other milestone, I will work you through this process. However, once you have managed to get through this stage, everything will be easier.

Today, with millions of websites online, it has become increasingly difficult for new businesses to appear on the first page of search engine results. You can't rely solely on search engine traffic when you're just starting. You have to find other ways to drive potential customers to your website.

Just to clarify, when we say "driving traffic to your website," note that this could be to any destination you wish to send people to. I highly recommend that you create your website, as it will be yours and you'll be in control of what happens there. Your website is like your home and traffic is like inviting people to come to pay a visit.

However, instead of "website", we could also use the term "platform," as it could be a podcast that you host, a YouTube channel, an Etsy store where you sell products, or anywhere else you wish to drive traffic.

Now, let's see what can be done to attract some eyeballs to your platform or wherever you wish to send visitors to engage with your offer.

Think of the ideal customer's avatar and channel what you offer towards them such that it gains their attention.

Aim for "Quality" Traffic which can be measured through engagement (visitors commenting on and sharing your blog posts), Conversion (visitors subscribing to your email list, or ending up, at some point, buying your product or service), and Brand advocates (visitors talking about you to their friends and ac□uaintances)

You have to reach the people who are most likely to be interested in your content, posts, videos, audio and in buying your product or service. These people are your target audience.

Your website should contain at least three to four sections if you have a blog, and five if you also have a product to sell.

1. *Homepage*; your homepage should clearly state what you're offering information on your product or service and whom the offer is for.

2. *About page*; this section contains information on you and your business, but more specifically about what you offer.

3. *Contact page*; this section gives the visitors a way to contact you for more information.

4. *Blog section*; your website might be a blog or contain a blog section, where you'll publish articles, videos, or content in other formats. In that case, it should contain at least a few articles.

5. *A sales page*; if you already have a product or service to sell, you should also have a sales page in place.

**Traffic Sources**

When you're just starting out, trying to be everywhere is overwhelming and unnecessary. After going through the list below, choose a few traffic-generation methods maybe two or three that could attract the highest number of quality visitors to your site. Make sure to use the 80/20 rule. What are the 20% of all traffic sources that will potentially bring you 80% of your highly targeted visitors? You can always expand your efforts later. It's better to promote through a few channels, rather than make an average effort in many channels. Choose the best traffic sources according to your topic, your niche, and the nature of your product or service.

**Here's an example that illustrates this idea:**

A friend of mine recently started creating jewelry and selling it on the Internet through a store on Etsy.com. Her jewelry is delicate, made of gold and silver, and is sold for between $15 and $50 per piece. Her target audience is middle-class women between the ages of 25 and 40 who like low-cost accessories.

Where should she primarily promote her product? Probably on Facebook, Pinterest and fashion blogs. She should create a Facebook page because it's the social media platform with the most users, and should rarely be ignored. There's also an Etsy app that she could add to her Facebook page to send visitors directly to her Etsy store. Facebook also allows posts with large images, which is good for a product that's easily communicated visually.

It would be almost impossible to ignore Pinterest. Pinterest's audience is made up of roughly 70% women, it's a visual medium, and it has a high sales conversion rate (the percentage of people who buy a product after visiting the platform). The pinned images are clickable, which makes it possible to send traffic directly to her website or Etsy.com.

Finally, she should consider approaching fashion bloggers. Since jewelry is an accessory that complements clothing well, she could propose a partnership and be featured on a fashion blog. This would be targeted, as there is a good chance that people who visit fashion blogs are interested in jewelry, as well. It would also be less expensive to create these partnerships with other bloggers in her industry than to advertise on high-traffic websites. With just these three traffic sources, she could probably reach a good number of potential buyers.

***Strategies that drive traffic to your website; choose the best options for your business.***

1. Guest post on other blogs; this implies writing and publishing an article on someone else's blog or website. The goal is to write for a blog that has a medium-to-large audience that corresponds with your target customers. You get exposure in front of a new audience with the aim of growing your business.

2. Accept guest writers on your blog; another way to increase your exposure and gain traffic is by allowing another person to write an article on your website. This time, the topic of the article must be interesting to your audience.

3. Get interviewed on podcasts to reach your target audience.

4. Interviewing an expert in your field is a great strategy to generate traffic, build relationships with influencers, and gain authority in your field.

5. Host webinars to promote a product, to generate sales, or to build an audience. They can be free, or imply a cost to attend.

6. Build a community on social media. Remember to choose the media that are the most relevant to your audience, your topic, and the nature of your product or service. Social media platform you can use include Facebook, Pinterest, Quora, Reddit, Instagram, Linkedin, Youtube, Tiktok.

7. SlideShare Presentations can be used for brand awareness which can then attract user's attention

8. Social Bookmarking Sites; if you have a blog, you could submit your articles to bookmarking sites like Delicious.com, Digg.com and StumbleUpon.com. The community vote on the □uality of your article will give you a chance to appear on the front page of the platform which will likely drive tons of traffic to your site.

9. Search Engine Optimization (SEO); while it's true that you can't rely solely on search engines to drive traffic to your website, especially at the beginning, that doesn't mean you shouldn't already optimize the aspects you have control over to increase your site's chances of eventually appearing in search engine results. This process is part of "search engine optimization" (SEO). Mainly, SEO can be divided into two categories: on-site and off-site. The part you have the most control over is your on-site optimization. This is everything you can do to your website itself to rank better including choosing the right keywords.

### *Don't Forget Your Main Goal*

Always remember your main goal when driving traffic to your website: building your email list. You should be sending traffic to a page with the best chances of converting visitors into subscribers on your email list. This could increase the conversion into subscribers by up to 10 times.

Whether you publish an article on a popular blog, are interviewed in a podcast, or promote yourself on social media, remember your main objective and choose to send people to a s□ueeze page designed for this purpose, rather than linking to your homepage or an article on your site.


*NETWORK WITH PEOPLE*

Building relationships with people in your field is also very important to grow your business. These relationships can be even stronger if you meet in person. There are several ways and occasions to meet influential people: through mentorship, by being part of a mastermind group, and by attending live events, such as conferences, seminars and Meetup events.

There is a community of strong single moms' platform that are willing to support other single moms by sharing their knowledge through conferences, forums and free resources. Connect with them and many other people that can support your business.

### Mentorship

Everyone could benefit from access to a more knowledgeable person for advice, feedback and guidance. Having the guidance of a mentor can prevent many mistakes from being made by the mentee (you) and provide shortcuts through the process of building your online business.

### Mastermind Groups

A mastermind group is a small group of people ideally three to five in the same field who meet regularly to talk about their projects, give and get advice and feedback, shares their struggles and hold each other accountable. This is an excellent way to meet like-minded people and build long-term relationships, as well as to get support in building and growing your business. Think of it as an opportunity to exchange information, experience, and expertise, as well as to create partnerships.

### Events

There are many live events, conferences, and seminars related to online business and fashioned towards single moms. You can find most of these events that are more specific to your topic and niche in a simple Google search. There are conferences for food bloggers, eCommerce businesses, authorpreneurs, mompreneurs etc.

### MeetUp.com

Meetup events are a great and easy way to meet and connect with people in your industry. Member of a group have varying levels of expertise. You could find a mentor, form a mastermind group with other members, create partnerships, and get access to several other opportunities.

# CHAPTER TEN

*STEP NINE: GENERATE* REVENUE

At first, you might have thought that creating and selling products would be the most challenging aspect of an online business, but don't worry. it's not.

You've already done most of the work by finding a topic and a niche, defining your audience, creating your ideal customer's avatar, generating traffic to your website and building an email list. That was the hardest part of building your business. Afterwards, creating and selling products or services should be quite easy at least it is in the digital world.

The type of products or services you can offer is almost unlimited. We'll cover a few of the most important ones and we'll mention a few resources to help you in the process.

### *Freelancing*

Freelancers are self-employed individuals who sell work or services by the hour or by job completion, rather than working on a regular salary basis for one employer.

As a freelancer, you can offer your services through your website or marketplace platforms, such as; Upwork.com, Freelancer.com, Guru.com, Freelance.com, PeoplePerHour.com, WeWorkRemotely.com and many more.

As a freelancer, you can bid on the jobs posted on the site or be directly contacted for a specific project. Usually, the intermediary service the freelancing platform gets a percentage of the total revenue generated for a job.

You can also offer your services through your website, but there needs to be more promotional effort made. In this case, all of the tactics mentioned in the preceding chapter about driving traffic to your site can be used to promote your freelancing services.

If you manage to build a team of complementary talents, you could take on more complex projects and share the revenues with your team members. You could also delegate some parts of a project by hiring people, or even delegate the whole process and act as a project manager. You can find team members through freelancing marketplaces or within Facebook and LinkedIn groups.

Finally, creating and selling online courses or eBooks that teach elements related to your field of expertise could add new and more passive income streams to your freelancing revenue.

### Online Coaching or Consulting

Online coaching or consulting can be offered in addition to in-person services. It primarily enables the consultant to work with clients located remotely and to work from home or anywhere else. It eliminates the distance barrier with potential clients. Sessions can be conducted through Skype, Google Hangouts, among other services.

Some great ways to promote your coaching and consulting service include guest posting on other blogs, self-publishing eBooks on Amazon Kindle, and hosting webinars.

By tackling a specific problem expressed within your niche market and providing some elements of a solution, you can promote your services as a more in-depth solution at the end of a webinar. You'll easily find the most urgent pain or desires of your target audience by looking at forums related to your topic.

Depending on your industry, there are also intermediary platforms, or directories, where you can offer your consulting services, such as; Clarity.fm for Business consulting and LifeCoachOnDemand.com for Life coaching

### Selling Other People's Products (Affiliate Marketing)

You can make a commission on others' products that you sell when you're enrolled in their affiliate program. You promote their products using an affiliate link provided by the advertiser. This link is only for you to use and will tell the advertiser that you made the sale. After clicking on the link, the visitor will be sent to the product's sales page. If the product is then purchased, you'll get a commission.

You should only recommend excellent products that will be useful to your audience. It is your responsibility to ensure that your product is of great

□uality. Promote products from people you know and/or have personally used and liked. Recommending a bad product, or one that wouldn't be useful to your audience would harm the trust they have in you. This hard-to-build trust is crucial to the relationship you have with your audience.

If there's a product you would like to sell to your audience, you can contact the company directly and ask to become a partner. Another way to find affiliate products is by searching on intermediary platforms that connect advertisers and publishers, such as ClickBank.com, JvZoo.com, cj.com and Amazon.com (affiliate-program.amazon.com)

Don't forget that you must let people know when a product you are recommending is an affiliate. You could simply say "here is my affiliate link for this product" and tell them that buying from this link helps you, at no extra cost to them.

*CREATING AND SELLING YOUR PRODUCTS*

There is a big difference between selling physical products online and selling digital products. The costs associated with production, stocking and delivery are non-existent for digital products but can be considered for physical ones.

**Types of Digital Products**

The most profitable model is usually creating and selling your digital products. Once you have properly defined your niche market and found your audience's pain and desires, you are well e☐uipped to design the best product to solve this pain.

The most common formats to present solutions are courses, eBooks, online live events (webinars), membership sites, audio tracks, software and digital magazines.

***Online Courses and Training***

If you have knowledge and information that could be useful to others, you should consider packaging it into an online course. It could be produced in a video, audio, or written format, or even a combination of them. A course should teach the audience how to achieve a specific objective. Courses can be created around almost any topic, as long as there are enough people interested in learning what you intend to teach.

If you already have an email list of a few hundred or more engaged subscribers, it would be advantageous to sell your course through your website or to host it on a platform such as Teachable.com, which facilitates the process of building the course and delivering the content to your audience. You could also allow others to promote the course for you by becoming affiliates.

If you don't have an audience yet but have the knowledge to share, you could offer your digital course through intermediary platforms, such as Udemy.com, SkillShare.com and Lynda.com. The profit margin will be lower since the intermediary will take a percentage, but it can be a great way to start since you'll have access to the platform's audience.

If the creation of an online video course intimidates you, know that there are many resources available to help you. Udemy.com offers a free class for aspiring instructors (Teach.Udemy.com) that explains the process of creating a course, including the technical and marketing aspects. You can also become a member of their Facebook group for instructors, where you can ask questions to a supportive community of online teachers. Even if you decide to sell your course on your website, those free Udemy resources can be very helpful.

There are also plugins you can install on your WordPress website that facilitate the task of creating and delivering a course. Some of these plugins are: ZippyCourses, TeachPress, Sensei, LearnDash

To build your course efficiently, break the information down into chunks and place it in a logical se□uence to ensure a good understanding by the audience. Start by giving an overview of the learning process, introducing the problem you propose to solve, as well as the solution offered, along with the benefits associated. Then, present the process, step-by-step, from the current problematic situation to achieving the result benefits.

### *EBooks*

Writing and self-publishing an eBook can not only help you gain more authority in your field, facilitate connections with influencers, and increase your reach and exposure, but it can also generate a significant income.

Until you have collected a considerable amount of email subscribers to your list, you'll probably want to take advantage of the Amazon Kindle self-publishing platform. This may surprise you, but there are individuals making a very good living writing and self-publishing eBooks.

However, once you've grown an email list of over 1,000 engaged subscribers, it becomes even more interesting, since you then have an audience to sell your eBooks to directly. You don't have to share the revenue with an intermediary and can start making a more substantial income from your books.

### *Webinars*

As the webinar organizer or host, you simply share information and knowledge that's useful for an audience that pays to receive it. You can be the one delivering the content, or you can find an expert to do so. For the latter, you would simply share the revenues with the expert, or pay him/her a fixed fee upfront.

Webinars can also be a great way to collect information about your audience. While presenting the content, attendees will ask □uestions, which can help you identify their main difficulties and desires. This is very valuable information that you can use to create another live event, or even a course or an eBook to sell. You could also decide to host a free webinar and use the occasion to sell another product.

### *Membership Sites*

On membership sites, members pay a recurring fee to have access to content, information, knowledge and advice that you provide. The fee is usually monthly but could be annually, bi-annually, or on any other basis you think is most suitable to the topic of your site.

This business model is especially suitable for topics that re□uire a long period of study. For example, guitar classes could be a good fit for a membership site, since it takes some time for a person to progress from a beginner to an expert level. The learning process can take several months, from learning the fundamental basics of guitar playing to gaining the capacity to play more complex melodies.

With a membership site, you'll have to deliver content regularly to justify the recurring fee. It would be a good idea to have several pieces of content, enough for the first month or two, ready by the time you launch your site.

### *Audio*

Audio products may include audiobooks, paid podcasts, music, meditation tracks, etc. They can be sold and downloaded directly from your website or through platforms like iTunes, Audible.com, SongCastMusic.com and Gumroad.com, among others. The sound □uality for this format is crucial, so make sure that you use a good microphone and reduce ambient sound as much as possible.

### *Digital Magazines*

With the rise of the popularity of mobile devices, digital magazines are another interesting product to create. Plus, there are now software solutions that make the magazines very easy to build. Two of such software products are Magcast.co and InHouseDigitalPublishing.com. To generate revenue, you can charge a subscription fee and sell advertising space to other businesses.

### *LEAN STARTUP*

When you plan on creating a product, it is a good idea to take the lean startup approach. Start by making a "minimum viable" version of the product, introduce it to your niche market, and observe the response before spending time, money, and effort on a more complex project.

For example, if you're planning to write a 200-page eBook, why not begin by writing a 30-page, less detailed version of it? Or try a couple of blog posts on the same topic, to publish on your website or someone else's, and observe if it triggers engagement?

For online courses, you could use a platform such as Udemy.com to release a shorter, less complex version of a course you would like to create and see what the response is.

## PRE-SELLING THE PRODUCT

Some entrepreneurs will choose to pre-sell their product before it's even created to make sure there will be buyers. They simply announce the product, say that it will be available on date X, and allow people to pre-order it. If there are buyers, the entrepreneur will immediately begin production.

If you decide to use this strategy, make sure that you've given yourself enough time to create the product when setting the launch date. You should have a plan and everything to start building it on hand.

## PRODUCT VALIDATION USING WEBINARS

Before creating a product, you could prepare a webinar on the same topic and see if there are people interested in attending. If you get a few attendees, it's a good sign that people are willing to learn about the subject and that there could potentially be buyers for a paid product. Webinars can also be an opportunity to pre-sell your product.

## DON'T WAIT TOO LONG BEFORE SELLING SOMETHING

One mistake many people make when they are just starting is waiting too long before offering a paid product. Often, they wait out of fear of a negative response from their audience. "Will they get mad at me because I'm selling something?"

Well, there will always be some individuals who complain, and yes, some will react negatively to the offer of a paid product. Does it matter? It shouldn't. The audience members who are complaining are not your ideal customers, and you do not want them as part of your audience. Let them be, and let them go. You can't possibly please everyone, so don't waste your energy in attempting to do so.

By getting your audience accustomed to being offered paid products or services early, you'll diminish the risk of a negative response later, as it won't take them by surprise. Within the first few emails of the series you send to new subscribers, you could include an offer as simple as a book recommendation for which you are an affiliate.

*Remember, you have got to be at peace with your self if you have gone this far. Trust me you are a winner*

# CHAPTER ELEVEN

*STEP TEN: THE PRICING STRATEGY*

T he price is a characteristic of your product. It is part of its branding and also of its market positioning, its place in the market compared to other similar offers (competitors).

Pricing is, therefore, an important element to consider when you build your business, not only as a mean of generating revenues but also as an element that impacts how your product will be perceived by potential consumers.

Pricing is often an element of discomfort among new entrepreneurs. Likely caused by a lack of experience and thus confidence, putting a price on a new product or service can make many new business owners nervous.

Many entrepreneurs don't know how much to charge and aren't sure of the value of the new product. They might also fear the market's reaction. Will they think the price is too high? What if they leave a comment on the web saying, "It certainly wasn't worth the cost!"?

***However, remember the definition of a business: getting remunerated for the value you bring to a market. There shouldn't be any shame in getting paid for providing value.***

If you keep your price low because of a lack of confidence in your product, it will show. The price of a product is often associated with its (perceived) quality. If you think that by offering your product at a very low price, you'll avoid potential complaints and will navigate in a safer zone, don't be so sure. Your displayed price should be in accordance with the benefit you are promising.

Your chosen positioning strategy in the market should also have an influence when determining the price, as it is one element that consumers will use to evaluate your offer. Whatever price you are willing to let your product sell for, there should be a good reason to back it up. A lower price isn't necessarily a bad thing, as long as you justify it. The same is true for a higher price.

If you wish to gain credibility, then the money isn't the main goal, either. You shouldn't settle for a very low or very high price, but more for something in the middle. However, if you want to generate revenue, then yes, you should aim for a higher price.

### The Paying Capacity of Your Target Market

If you've done some research into your avatar's (ideal customer's) profile, you should have an idea about its income, its discretionary budget, and its willingness to pay for the type of product you are offering. If your target market is single parents on benefits or college students, and you're selling a giant home cinema screen, there's a good chance that this market, even if interested in your offer, won't have the ability to pay for it.

This is an important aspect to consider when deciding on a niche. Ideally, you want to serve a market that has discretionary income to spend on non-essential goods.

### The Market's Reference Price

This should also be a good indicator. Look at your competitors' product characteristics and related pricing. Compare the characteristics of their offer versus yours. Then, think of the position in the market that you would like to occupy. Are you a low-cost, average, or high-end option?

### Cover Your Costs

If you write a book, your fixed cost will include the production of your book, including the writing time, the cover illustration, the editing, and proofreading. The variable cost will include the printing and distribution fees per book.

Unless you've decided to give your product away for free, you'll want to cover both your fixed and variable costs. If the purpose of creating your product is to generate revenue, then you may want to sell it for at least three times its variable cost of production. On the other hand, if the purpose is to generate leads (subscribers), then you might not need to cover your costs since it will be considered more as an investment.

### The Perceived Value of the Benefit Your Customers Will Gain After Consuming Your Product

The benefits to be gained by using the product, and the effort re□uired, should be considered when deciding on the product's price. For example, how much would a person who wants to lose ten pounds to look great before the summer be willing to pay for a weight loss program? What about a woman who wants to fit into her wedding dress? Or a man who needs to lower his cholesterol to avoid imminent health problems?

Your target market will be more or less sensitive to a price depending on the importance of overcoming the "pain" as well as its urgency.

Also, what will it take for your customers to overcome the "pain"? If you're offering a weight loss program that guarantees good results within two months by following an exercise and healthy cooking plan, how much would the average person who wants to lose weight □uickly be ready to pay? How much would that same person be willing to pay for a simple, natural pill that guarantees the same results? Probably more than the exercise plan, as the effort required for achieving the result is smaller.

Marie Forleo, a business coach and entrepreneur, has a great way of explaining the perceived value of a product: *The Mattress Method*. Can you translate the value of your product into real-life currency, like time, money, love, and health?

She gives an example of the day she went shopping for a new mattress. The mattress she was looking at was more expensive than other types offered on the market, but the salesman reminded her that: You spend one-third of your time in bed. Good sleep improves your productivity, health, and good looks

Essentially, the salesman told her that good sleep contributed to making her richer, healthier, and prettier. These are the tangible benefits of the product in real-life currency. What is the perceived value of the benefits your customers will gain after purchasing your product?

### The Portfolio of Products

You should offer multiple levels of products or services. For example, if you have an eBook selling for $19, an online course at $79, and a one-hour consultation at $250, you have a portfolio of three products. Offering multiple levels of products gives people a price reference point.

In the example above, if you only sell an eBook and an online course, the online course may be perceived by consumers as too expensive, but when you add a pricier item the $250 consultation to the portfolio, it makes the middle offer seem more affordable. It's psychological. Most people will opt for the middle option.

Another reason to consider a product portfolio is that some people will only want the high-end option. If you don't offer a high-end option or a more expensive product, they will buy one elsewhere.

In the book 80/20 Sales and Marketing, Perry Marshall explains that there will always be people willing to buy a very expensive offer. He gives the example of Starbucks. Starbucks sells cups of regular filter coffee for $2.50. You can also buy a complete breakfast for about $12, including a soy latte, biscotti, and a fruit salad. But have you noticed the espresso machine also available for sale? Of course, not many customers will buy the $400 espresso machine, but a few will. If Starbucks didn't offer an espresso machine, the customer who wanted to buy one would get it from somewhere else. Starbucks would lose a sale for not offering the product.

Do you have a high-end product to offer? If not, can you create one? Not only will offering one make your other, lower-cost products look more affordable to your customers' eyes, but not offering one will most likely cause you to lose potential sales.

The bottom line is to offer multiple levels of products or services. It helps people to make a purchase decision when they can compare products and prices.

*RESIST THE DISCOUNT URGE*

Discounted rates are addictive. When people see your product offered at a discount, they'll have a harder time buying it at the regular price later. They may expect further discounts and wait for one before buying. Plus, discounting can evoke confusion towards the perceived quality of the product you are offering. If it's sold for less, does that mean it's worth less than what it was previously offered for?

The ⬚uestion is: What should you do instead?

A better approach is to add extra value for a limited time. In the context of launch, this may include adding another item to the original offer as a bonus. For example, if you're selling an online course on outdoor photography, you could offer a free eBook on how to take great sunrise and sunset shots to the first 10 buyers.

If your product is a book, you could offer the audio version at no extra fee, for a limited number of copies sold or for a limited time. It's a bargain for your audience without diminishing the perceived value of your main product or accustoming consumers to discounted prices. Note that the bonus item should be relevant to the main product and, ideally, should complement it.

*Bottom line is that there will always be unhappy people, and that's okay. Live with it, and stop being scared of putting a price on your product. That said, if the complaints you're getting with regards to your product's price are generalized, maybe you did do something wrong. In that case, listen to the constructive negative feedback, and, if possible, modify your price accordingly.*

# CHAPTER TWELVE

Two main elements play a huge role in convincing potential customers to consider your offer. One is the trust they have in you as a person, and the other is the confidence they have that the product will solve their problem. It is important to know that trust is not the same as manipulation.

If you want to build honest and lasting relationships with your buyers then trust is very essential. You do have a genuine desire to serve your market and help them solve their problem, and sincerely believe that your product or service can solve it, right? In that case, you simply have to find the best way to tell them.

Persuasion is often synonymous with the power of influence, and can even be associated with seduction and manipulation.

In the context of selling your product or service, however, it's more about convincing your potential customers of your offer's real capacity to solve their problem. This is a very important step that can determine how many sales you will make. If you genuinely believe in the value of your product and the positive impact it will have on your target market, you should definitely be e□uipped to share its benefits with potential customers.

### The Main Elements That Contribute To Persuading Others

These factors can and should be used on your website, mainly on your product sales page, and even on your About page.

*Reciprocation*: You probably have a friend who once paid for the two beers you had at the bar, even though it wasn't your birthday or any other special occasion. Perhaps it surprised you, and you felt a mixture of gratitude and discomfort. Maybe you told yourself or even your friend that next time, drinks would be on you. The law of reciprocation stipulates that when someone does us a favor, we feel the obligation to return it. Until we do so, we feel a kind of discomfort we owe something. You have probably heard marketers say that you should give tons of value to your audience before asking for anything. Once you've given your audience value (free content, video courses, eBooks, blog posts, etc.), they will most likely be willing to buy your paid product in the future. Not only will they trust you, but they might also feel the need to reciprocate and give back to you. Give and you shall receive.

*Credibility*: Credibility is about demonstrating your expertise on a topic. It's about showing your competence to solve your audience's problem. Do you have a diploma? Display it. Wrote a book on the topic? Add a link to it. Have worked many years in the field? Explain that in your bio. If you have good knowledge on a topic, years of practice in the field, or any other type of authority, it'll be easier to convince people that you can help them solve their problem. It will enhance your authority. Show your credentials, diplomas, experience, and authority title. It will make people more confident that you are the best person to help them.

*Commitment and Consistency*: When we commit to doing something, we naturally feel obligated to keep our word, or we feel at fault. **The law of consistency** refers to your audience's need to keep their commitments. For example, if you ask your audience whether they would buy a certain product if you created it for them, the ones who answer "yes" may feel the obligation to be consistent and commit to their word by buying the product once it's released.

*Liking*: People prefer to say 'yes' to those they know and like. That's kind of obvious. Would you buy a product, a painting, or a coaching session from someone you dislike, if someone you liked better offered an e□uivalent? Probably not. The □uestion, then, is how do we make people like us?

*According to research by Cialdini's, we tend to like people: Who are similar to us, Share our values, background, current situation, Who cooperate with us in a common goal, Work with us as a team, or share our vision, Who have complimented us and Who make us feel good about ourselves.*

Dave Kerpen, the author of Likeable Business, states that what is critical in building a following is to first make sure that people know you, second, that they like you, and third, that they trust you.

Liking is at the center of building relationships, and for it to happen, people need to know you and connect with you. Then, to become followers or customers, they also need to trust you. There is no shortcut for this.

Here is where knowing your audience well and feeling empathy for them will be particularly handy. If you can demonstrate to your audience that you understand their situation because you've also been there and remember how it was, they will feel a deeper connection to you. They'll relate to you.

People who share your values will also connect with you more easily. They will see what you stand for by reading your organization's mission statement or hearing your elevator pitch and tagline, and those who feel touched and concerned about your vision will more easily become buyers of your products and services.

You also should tell your audience that you will be working with them towards achieving their goals and that their well-being is also your concern. Also, giving genuine compliments on their improvements, the choices they made, and their perseverance can also boost your likeability, as you'll make them feel good about themselves.

***Social Proof and Consensus***: We usually feel better making a decision others have made, the same choice or taken the same action. It validates our behavior and makes us feel more confident that we made the right decision.

Also, it's been shown that people trust recommendations from peers more than from any other sources. According to a study by Nielsen in 2009 "Recommendations from personal ac□uaintances or opinions posted by consumers online are the most trusted forms of advertising. Ninety per cent of consumers surveyed noted that they trust recommendations from people they know, while 70 per cent trusted consumer opinions posted online."

This means that people will be keener and feel more reassured about buying your product if they see that others have also bought it, and even more so if other buyers have expressed their satisfaction and written a great product review. Therefore, adding testimonials from real buyers to your website especially on the product sales page should have a positive impact on the number of sales.

Another way you can make people more comfortable with buying your product is to highlight popular items. You can tell them what the most popular choice is, or simply mention how many people have purchased the product.

**The law of social proof and consensus** also affects social sharing and liking. People are usually keener on sharing content that has already been shared by others and like a page that is very popular (has many fans).

*Scarcity*: Along with social proof, scarcity is probably the element that will help you the most in increasing sales. Scarcity refers to a limited □uantity of an offer. If your offer is a service, it's possible that there are limited places available, and this is very understandable.

Scarcity is also very conceivable for a physical product, people can't order a product that's out of stock. In those cases, you can easily mention that people should register or buy as soon as possible because availability is limited.

For digital products like online courses or eBooks, you could offer bonus items for the first few purchases. Bonus items can be an audio version of your book, access to a higher level course, a one-on-one consulting session, or anything that is perceived as valuable by your audience.

*PERSUASION TIPS TO INCREASE YOUR PRODUCT SALES*

### Address Objections

Objections are reasons why a potential buyer may hesitate on the purchase. You'll convince your audience to buy your product or service more easily if you address their objections before they even have time to come up with them, by providing counterarguments to these objections.

Here are some examples of objections: "I don't know if I'll be able to create a website. I'm a real dummy with computers!", "I don't have time.", "and it's a little expensive for my budget."

**Counterarguments**:

"I'll show you the whole process, step-by-step, in such a simple way that even your grandmother could do it!", "You can take the course at your own pace with only two hours per week. In two months, you'll know enough Spanish vocabulary and verbs to speak to the hotel staff on your vacation.", "Using your new skill acquired from the course, you will recover your investment within two weeks."

Objections are usually related to time, money, or confidence in whether the product will help them solve their problem or satisfy their needs. Note that

78

using your audience's expressions and language style when mentioning the objections will work best.

### The Loss and the Gain

You must also mention what people will gain by consuming your products (benefits), or even what they'll lose by not doing so. There are two types of motivational focus: prevention focus and promotion focus.

People who are more of the "prevention" type tend to be more sensitive towards what they could lose. They want to be safe. As for people who are more of the "promotion" type, they will be more sensitive to what they could gain, or to opportunities.

On a product sales page, you should use both "loss" and "gain" motivation tactics, since the page will be promoting to a large number of people of potentially both types.

### Offer a good guarantee

A guarantee lowers the buyer's anxiety. It diminishes the doubts the customer might have about purchasing by knowing that, if he isn't satisfied with the product, he can get a full refund within the following week or month.

If you think that offering such guarantees will make you lose money because some people will ask for a refund, don't worry. First, if you offer a good guarantee, a lot more people will buy your product. Second, if your product is good, very few will ask for a refund.

### USE PERSUASION TECHNIQUES ON YOUR ABOUT PAGE

The primary goal of your About page isn't to generate sales, but it is a great place to use some of the persuasion principles to increase your influence.

### Here's how to use them:

### Liking

The approach you take in writing your About page will differ depending on your industry and on the product or service you're offering. Just remember, it has to be about them first. Clearly mention what's in it for them using an empathic approach.

### Reciprocation

You can give more details about what they'll find on your website. If there's a blog, tell them about the valuable content you'll be providing consistently. Mention the great tips and the helpful information they'll get through your site. They'll be grateful for your help, and, hopefully, have this in mind when you promote a paid product.

### *Credibility*

Now you can insert your credentials. Reassure your audience that you're the ideal person to serve them by showing your expertise on the topic i.e. your experience in the field and your credentials.

If you have a considerable following on social media, you can display your content count for likes and shares by using Facebook like a box. You could also add social proof facts, such as: "More than fifty people have had excellent results using our service" or "Subscribe to our email list and join a community of more than 10,000 members."

If your site is new and you don't have much of a following or many subscribers (or any at all), you could ask someone you know who has benefited from your product or service to write a testimonial, which you can display at the end of your About page or in the right sidebar.

With only a few tweaks to your About page, you'll inspire trust from your audience, which is a primary re□uirement for them to become customers.

# CHAPTER THIRTEEN

*GIVE AWAY: RAISE FUNDS FOR YOUR ONLINE BUSINESS*

As your business grows, raising funds becomes essential to run your business especially if you have a product to launch to your audience market. It's not enough to have a great idea. While you might be able to bootstrap your businesses, many entrepreneurs will need outside funding to start (or grow) their businesses.

You might get lucky and raise start-up capital from venture capital firms. But the vast majority of founders raise the initial funding for their business from friends and family, or investors, wealthy individuals who fund new startups and believes in your business.

***To improve your chances to raise funds from any possible source, consider the following tips.***

### Have a Plan

Your plan does not need to be a formal, 100-page document. It can be a simple PowerPoint or Keynote presentation. The act of writing a plan forces you to crystallize your thoughts and to make sure that you could articulate your ideas succinctly, accurately, and with sufficient detail. It also forces you to thoroughly research the market and competitors.

Include a good description of your business, light financial projections, and competitive market analysis. We will dig deeper into this aspect in the latter part of this book

### Research

As mentioned earlier in the book, know your business and market as well as your competitors. Most investors are smart people. They'll want to know about your idea, the potential market, the competitors, the pitfalls, etc. While it's impossible to prepare to answer every single ▢uestion, you should try to learn as much as you possibly can so that you are ready. Potential investors will ▢uickly tune you out if you can't answer key ▢uestions about your business.

### Practice

Find the smartest people you can and persuade them to be brutally honest with you. You'll appreciate this later, even if you're uncomfortable about this initially. Pitch your idea to those people and then listen carefully to their feedback. Be honest and don't hide things. Be sure that in your written materials as well as in your oral presentations, you are fully transparent about your business, what you're looking to do, and what you want from investors.

### Crowdfunding

You can also consider raising money from your friends, family, members, customers or clients through crowdfunding sites like Kickstarter.com, Indiegogo.com or Peerbackers.com. You can ask for a specific amount of money and in return for the donations received, offer prizes to reward those who believe in you.

### Find the right investors.

This is easier said than done. For many new businesses, any investor is the right investor. But some investors will make you miserable. It's always a good idea to look for experienced investors. Novice investors may demand a lot of attention, and this becomes very difficult when you are trying to run your company.

### Limit the number of investors.

If you have too many investors, you'll have to manage many relationships and expectations. While for some, there is no way around it, try to keep the number of investors under two dozen.

### Prepare legal documents.

If you are asking others, especially strangers, to give you lots of money, don't be surprised that they'll want to see e▢uity financing documents. And you don't want to start thinking about such documents too late in the capital-raising process. The most important take-away: when an investor indicates their interest, have your e▢uity financing documents ready. Don't ask them to wait.

### Keep working on your new business

Raising capital takes a lot of time. During the time that you raise capital, you must remember to keep working on your business. If you focus solely on raising capital and ignore your idea, you not only run the risk of failure but your investors and potential investors will wonder whether you will be able to complete your seed round and launch your company. You must find a way to do both.

### Don't take rejection personally.

In all aspects of the business. Don't take rejection personally. People will decline to invest for many reasons. Some won't see much merit in your idea. Others will think that you are inexperienced. Still, others might decline because the terms of the investment don't fit their investment re□uirements. Don't ignore rejection. Learn from it.

### Simplify negotiations with investors.

Instead of negotiating separate deals with each investor, figure out what share of your new business you would be comfortable selling in return for the investment. Then divide it proportionally based on the amount of the investment, so that each investor pays a proportional share for their interest.

Raising capital is hard. It re□uires a lot of preparation and effort. Many new businesses fail because they can't raise sufficient funding. It will be one of the most difficult things you'll ever do with your business. But it's not impossible if you properly prepare.

# CHAPTER FOURTEEN

*STEP TWELVE: CREATING GOALS*

Without goals, you will have no way to measure the success of your business. You also will have a harder time maintaining focus and working with the end in mind. A lot of hard work is going to be made before you see any sort of real progress. Goals will be your guide to success.

There are so many ways to measure the success of your business. A common measurement is in terms of income. However, in the beginning, I think measuring your success in income will only disappoint you. If you can accept the fact that it takes most new businesses a couple of months, at the very least, to generate profit then you will be able to stay on track much better. A better way of measuring success is by how well you are reaching your smaller goals.

***Other Ways of Measuring Success***

Blog/Website Visitors (Install Google Analytics to track this. It's a free service.)

Contact initiated by customers

Number of Clients

How Many Events you have booked

Use a form of measurement that aligns with your long term goals. And remember, everyone's definition of success is different.

Now to the fun part, let's talk about those long term goals.

***Long Term Business Goals***

The whole point of you starting this business is to make money. If you stick with your plan and idea you will make money, maybe even lots of it! So when coming up with your long term goals you have to decide how much money you need to make per month.

You can set a goal to make $1,200.00 per month from your blog after one year. In addition, you can set up mini-goals each month to gradually lead me up to your main goal. You may not always meet those goals but having them there will keep you motivated to push on.

You need to decide what amount of money makes the initial work worth it to you. Then you need to think of a time frame. It could be a year. I see a year as being a reasonable time frame and I am confident that your efforts and commitment will pay off. For you, a year may be too long. Make your decision. Ensure your plan reflect your decision. The more money you want to make and the faster you want to make it e□uals more work and a lot more marketing. Whatever decisions you make you need to create habits that will move you toward your goals.

*CREATE SUCCESS HABITS*

Goals are dreams we are working to accomplish. Habits are the stepping stones to accomplishing those dreams. With every goal, we are striving to accomplish there are many habits that we can develop to take us a step closer to accomplishing our dreams.

Goals are the motivation you need. They are the desired outcome. Habits are what it takes to reach your goals. Don't look at habits like bad things such as smoking or overeating. It's time to train your brain to learn new habits that will set you up for success.

**Three things to develop your habits.**

1. The first step may seem very obvious, but defining your goals and figuring out the "why" is the most important step.

2. Once you have concrete goals laid out and strong reasons why these goals are important to you, it's time to think of the habits you can develop to bring you closer to these goals.

3. To make these habits for success stick they have to be tracked. You've set your goals but can you define why you made them? Why do you want to start a side business? Everyone's answer will be different, but for a single mom

**THE BENEFITS OF HAVING AN ONLINE BUSINESS ARE TREMENDOUS AS A SINGLE MOTHER;**

You can spend more time at home with your kids instead of working excessive hours.

You can create something you can be proud of and earn an income from it

Your business may start as a side business, but has the potential to produce enough income to be a full-fledged business.

Since you know your goals you need to think of which habits will bring you closest to achieving them. Marketing related activities should be one of those habits. The core parts of running your business should also be the main focus.

*MAKE A LIST*

Make a list of all the habits you can develop that will bring you closer to your goal. Once you have your list try narrowing it down to the top two or three that will benefit you the most. You can concentrate on one at a time or both if you feel like you can handle it. Work hard on turning these activities into habits. Once you have these down you can move on to developing new success habits.

*KEEP TRACK*

The best way to ensure these success habits stick is by tracking them. Schedule time to work on these habits in your daily planner. Shoot for a specific amount of time to spend on each activity and specific days. Keep track of how well you are doing. If after four weeks the habits have not stuck consider adjusting your schedule up or down. You may be putting too much on your plate or you may be capable of doing more. Experiment until you find out what works the best for you. It will take a minimum of four weeks to turn a new activity into a habit.

Once you develop these habits you won't even have to think about marketing or remember to do an important task for your business. It will be second nature and you will have set yourself up for success!

STAY MOTIVATED

By now you should have a vision of what you want the end product of your business to look like. You have a long term goal and several short term goals that will help get you there. Since it may take a year or more to make real headway you need to keep yourself motivated.

Celebrating and recognizing small achievements will help keep you on track. Don't look at how far you have to go, always look at how far you have come. It's very easy to give up and lose hope. That's why it's important to pick a subject or niche in which you are interested in and to constantly remind yourself of why you are beginning this business in the first place.

There are many motivating factors for single moms. Your kids, finance and the naysayers (you've got to prove them wrong). Let these motivation factor be your driving force.

Be patient, continually strive to do better, and stay motivated. I know you can do it! Think of reasons that really motivate you to keep pushing on when you feel like giving up!

*Creating Goals and Habits*

*List all of your long term business goals. Picture yourself in a year from now. What does your business look like? List the habits you can develop that will bring you closer to your goal. Determine which days and how much time you will spend on developing these habits. Track your habits for a minimum of four weeks.*

KEEP GOING AND DON'T GIVE UP

*"The price of success is hard work, dedication to the job at hand, and the determination that whether we win or lose, we have applied the best of ourselves to the task at hand."*

*Vince Lombardi*

If you can stick it out through the first year you are on your way to success. The first year might be the toughest in terms of time and money. You will have your fair shares of struggles and self-doubt. There will be many times when you just want to quit. Don't □uit.

Successful businesses do not happen overnight. There are no get rich □uick tactics. If there were everyone would be rolling in money by now. For you to be successful you are going to have to put in the hard work and effort and have faith that with time your business will succeed.

When you finally start to reach the level of success you had hoped for you will begin to build momentum. With each month that passes you by you will find more clients and will make more money. And, eventually, you will hit your desired income goal.

When you make it to this point you will be so glad that you put the time and effort in to make your business succeed. You will have something to be very proud of. You will have less financial stress and hopefully, be able to free up additional time to spend with your family.

### Never Stop Learning

Even if you are able to reach your income goal □uicker than expected don't stop learning about your business. Technology and marketing methods are constantly changing. There is always something new to be learned. Read up on as many books and blogs that you can on the subject of your business. Make connections with other people who are more successful than you and take note of what they do. Constantly seek to improve.

The most successful people invest in themselves. They never stop learning and they aren't afraid to try new things. Study successful people and see if you can pick up some of their habits.

### Be Proud

I hope that this book has given you ideas of what you can do to start your side business and the courage to get started. The fear of failure is real, and it's scary. Don't let fear hold you back. Follow your heart and pursue an idea that means something to you. Start a business that you can be proud of.

Your journey might be long and hard. Accept the fact that it takes time to develop success and it takes time to build up clients. But it can be done and it can be done by you!

Never let negativity s□uash your chances for success. There are always a handful of doubters. They may think that you are crazy for spending so much time on a project that isn't bringing you immediate income. But it takes time!

My hope for you is that you will take action and turn your dream job into a reality. Keep learning about your craft, make connections with others who can help you, and keep going when the times get tough.

*In the end, you will be so glad you did.*

www.ingramcontent.com/pod-product-compliance
Lightning Source LLC
Chambersburg PA
CBHW021455210526
45463CB00002B/791